The Recovery of the Person

Carlyle Marney

Abingdon
Nashville

THE RECOVERY OF THE PERSON

ISBN-0-687-35610-5

Acknowledgment is hereby made to the following
publishers for permission to use copyrighted material:

The Macmillan Company for excerpts from *A Theology for the Social Gospel* by
Walter Rauschenbusch.

New Directions, for three lines from "Do not go gentle into that good night," by
Dylan Thomas, from *The Collected Poems of Dylan Thomas.*

MANUFACTURED BY THE PARTHENON PRESS AT
NASHVILLE, TENNESSEE, UNITED STATES OF AMERICA

to CHRIS and SUSAN

more or less patient teachers
on my road to personhood

Wherefore I do call upon thee, Lord God of Abraham, and God of Isaac, and God of Jacob and Israel, who art the Father of our Lord Jesus Christ; the God who, through the abundance of Thy mercy, hast had a favor toward us, that we should know Thee; who hast made heaven and earth, who rulest over all, who are the only and the true God, above whom there is none other God; grant by our Lord Jesus Christ, the governing power of the Holy Spirit, to every reader of this book to know Thee, that Thou art God alone, to be strengthened in Thee, and to avoid every heretical, and godless, and impious doctrine. —A Prayer of Irenaeus

Foreword

When *The Recovery of the Person* first appeared in 1963 I was a seminary student. It struck me then as both jarring and liberating. Its passionate review of continental liberalism—from its beginnings in Schleiermacher's response to Kant to its end in Barth's burial of Harnack and Troeltsch—drove me to study this nineteenth-century legacy. Marney fascinated me with the suggestion that Schleiermacher and Barth ironically converged in their christological foci because of a shared reticence about speaking of God as personal.

Affirming the objectivity of revelation and of the sovereign God, Carlyle Marney wrestles in this book with the question of how that objective reality becomes *subjective, personal* truth for us split and fractured moderns. He struggles to say how we are healed of our splitness and drawn into redeeming engagement with the inhumanity and lostness of our world. In doing so he presses toward a reclaiming of the concrete social-ethical imperatives of the coming kingdom of God.

Marney wrote as a theologian who had done his homework. He

was thoroughly at home in the Scriptures, in Patristics, and in the writings of the landmark figures from Augustine to Teilhard de Chardin. As did many of those men, Marney taught frequently in universities and seminaries. But also, like most of them, his main work consisted in the week-by-week responsibility of making the Word flesh in preaching and pastoral leadership. Few men ever worked harder at the task of preaching than did Marney. *The Recovery of the Person* is no merely academic treatment of theological themes. It is the anguished struggle of a great pastor-theologian at mid-career to find a way to help the church encounter afresh the revolutionary personal disclosure of the God who became like us. It is the powerfully honest confession of a pastor's disillusionment with the church's evasion of its redemptive participation in the mission of Jesus Christ.

Subtitled "A Christian Humanism," this book centers on one bracing issue: What if in the incarnation God really did give *us* the privilege and burden of being co-redemptors with Christ? What if our affirmations that only God will bring the kingdom, and that in his own time, are really pious denials of our vocation as responsible persons and Christians? If so, they become denials of the incarnation.

Marney's Christian humanism contains no glib optimism about human goodness. I know no pages in recent theology that speak more searingly of the brutal realities of human violence and evil. His sermon-poem based on Carl Sandburg's "Wilderness" graphically evokes the beast in our hearts and genes. The harsh beauty in this confrontation makes credible and powerful Marney's call to make our "passing through here" one which—with Jesus Christ—cuts cleansingly into the cumulative moral sourness of our shared history.

No panaceas here. Strong words against bad religion: "We keep expecting suffering to be vicarious and atonement to be painless. We deny our humanhood to escape his (Christ's) divinity" (p. 110). Marney gives us an incisive perspective after which we can not think of human life as without purpose. We are called to nothing less than co-redeemership with the incarnate, crucified One. Church is wherever that vocation is being taken up, and where persons—in obedient identification—are priesting others toward healing, wholeness, and justice.

The editors at Abingdon were considering the reprinting of *The Recovery of the Person* when Carlyle Marney died, July 3, 1978. It is fitting that this book, which stood at the center of his writing and represented the beginning of a significant turning in his ministry and theology, should be the first of his writings to be republished. I hope it is the first of many. A new generation—who sadly will not hear him in person—deserve to have access to the challenging honesty, the humanizing vision, and the great-hearted faithfulness of this best-all-round pastor-theologian I ever hope to know.

James W. Fowler

Dr. James W. Fowler is Associate Professor of Theology and Human Development at Candler School of Theology, Emory University, Atlanta, Georgia. He worked with Dr. Marney as Associate Director of Interpreters' House at its beginning.

Preface

This approach to an incarnational realism in ethics rests on a theology of identification. The implicit emphasis is a Christian humanism, once impertinent in the absence of a viable doctrine of God transcendent, but no longer premature. This Christian humanism, a cutting edge in theology, is neither new nor novel, and rises out of the dramatic excursus in theology of the last forty years. While it accepts that God is God and we are men, it insists that God the Father, the Son, and the Holy Spirit must be talked of in such human terms as to be thought of as Person. It sees that God who is God, who comes to us men, indeed has become one of us men, so much so as to love and need us men, now demands that his manward journey be met by the response of persons in obedience. Our journey of obedience to the light we have may or may not result in new light from God, but it does issue in that recovery of persons without which "redemption," "church," and "the renewal of the church by the Holy Spirit" are irrelevant referrents to a relation that had no real meaning. The church is the womb within which persons happen and recognize one another.

CARLYLE MARNEY

Contents

Introduction

The Urgent Personal

One day in a kind of fever, under pressure to furnish some kind of ending to *Structures of Prejudice,* I wrote what I thought was the end of the matter. I now discover it was the beginning of the Peyton Lectures, which, still feverish, I repeated at Princeton Seminary; but the theme, "The Recovery of the Person," still haunts me. I did not get done with it. Perhaps it is not unheard of that the closing phrases of one score should have provided a new beginning. Let me introduce, then, this attempt to approach the crux of Christian personhood with a revision of those earlier pages.

The fragmentation of modern man is an inescapable and primary effect of that fragmentation of the modern world which began centuries ago. This larger fragmentation, best seen in the work of Machiavelli, Descartes, Bacon, Adam Smith, and others, now appears as a feature of politics, philosophy, economics, education, and most any other division one could use for an approach to the discussion of life in general. Even, if not especially, in the educational factories there is a welter of various curricula, departments, graduate programs, and few can be said to be putting anything together; this is too bad. It means that most men will live out their lives under the blinding light of some little specialty and will never try to plumb the darkness of the great dark room. They will work in order not to work, ask only not to have to ask, and seek not to have to learn of the mighty contradictions that split us. We are fragmented, split off, and there is no healing for fragments. This is the essence of contradiction. The great quest becomes how to find the whole; is there a whole to be found?

With respect to this wholeness, given a decade out of the training compartments, a man ought to have become responsible for his own fragmented ignorance. He can no longer blame the school of his beginning because there will have been time enough and books enough and people enough and pain enough to teach him, if he will learn. Given a decade on the journey, even a Christian minister should have been able to forgive his teachers their trespasses and should have recognized that all any seminary could have given him is a set of tools with which to work.

On his own, he should know the agony of this world of split men who work under their bright lights on their tiny islands, never sensing the surrounding illimitable darkness. Such a man in such a world should have come to hurt for the hordes of sense-driven hive-dwellers who will never come to the tree in the midst of the garden. He should have been able to recognize how his church and himself are very great sinners, how helpless he is truly to reconcile, and he should have drunk deeply at least once of the sacramental wine of his own failure. By the time of his maturity he should know the lack of seriousness in the charge that any real thinker must abandon the church, for he will have discovered that there is no other place to go!

14

He should know by now that cynicism is homicidal, pride is egomania, and nihilism is for sophomores. He should have had to weep over some village he is too small to take, but he should have outrun the temptation to be a bourgeois messiah. He is able neither to abandon nor to join. He has neither the nerve to jump ship nor the innocence to sing in the choir. Yet a grace for mankind within him should let him see that there are no choirboy Antichrists, which should give him hope for the very young, at least. And he should have begun to recognize by now his allies: he should have discovered that even among those who delineate the roads to inferno there sometimes is to be seen a glimpse of a road to Damascus. He should have learned that those of the great church at God's left hand know about the gathered darkness, too. And when they charge that life, like Dutch landscapes, has nothing but horizontal lines, by their very humanistic negation they testify to the possibility that vertical lines wait to let more light into the frame. He should have sensed by now that revelation lies behind and flows through the revolution that now occupies his world.

With all this maturity wrapped up in one package a man would be ready for Kant's three questions: What can I know? What ought I to do? What can I hope? The answer, for Kant, seems to lie in the context of reason and experience within a community of inquiry. Very well, I will work with this—a community within which inquiry can happen— and I have been inquiring—since boyhood—what can I know, what ought I to do, what can I hope—and no school I know could give me these answers. Instead, were we all not introduced to a fantastic parade?

I

Here you must forgive an old seeker's nostalgia, for I have seen the parade and am still a seeker. For ten seasons, when my children were very young, we went to the corner by the governor's mansion to see the amazing crepe-paper-and-wire ingenuity of the spring parade at our university. After it had snaked its brilliant way by us, we hurried down to Congress Avenue to see it pass again. Now, at my age, I have been a seeker thirty-five of my years, a Don Quixote and a mimic; but for twenty of these years I have been chasing theologians in a fantastic parade. I have small-boyed my big-eyed way into the marchers surrounding half a hundred exhibits, but the parade has gone full circle, some of the mimers and *papier-mâché* constructions are passing me again, and I have my bewilderments.

I saw Schleiermacher out the back door of my seminary eighteen years after Barth buried him. But great Schleiermacher did not die. He went around the chapel and then home, as Kant used to do at commencement time to keep from hearing some very bad sermons. Now Schleiermacher is coming back in the front door again, as indeed he must, for has Barth not replaced his bust in the *lares* of the gods?

My set of Harnack—imported, if you please, and paid for with grocery money—and my Troeltsch and my Ritschl were passé, people said, when I got them. But you can buy Harnack for $2.40 in paperback; and behold, the timbers of Harnack, Troeltsch, and Ritschl lie visibly in the base of Richard Niebuhr's methodology of Christian ethics, and the same three can be felt in *The Prayers of Walter Rauschenbusch,* now reprinted.

In my own lifetime as a seeker, what was once Buttrick's "heresy" on atonement has become standard Reformed dogma. Harry Emerson Fosdick has gone a full and grand circle. Crawford Toy is revered at Louisville where he was once dismissed, and Gezork has his host of friends in a South that rejected him. Thomas Aquinas has been baptized a German Protestant; Pelagius appears again among the

16

educated Methodists; Plotinus moves lively now behind the pages of Karl Barth I have read; and Arius, who would have died eighteen hundred years ago if he had been properly appreciative of Bishop Alexander's preaching, Arius, who should never have been allowed to achieve the status of a heretic, is ancestor to the flowering of New England. He was never really camouflaged as a Unitarian. Ritschl's Christ, as having for Christians the value of God, rides, with the faint odor of docetic gnosticism, in the Trojan horse led by Bultmann, and the awful effort to evade the dread historicity of the gospel requires a whole calvacade of once-dead docetics to animate the three-story history they project. This metaphysical device, more complicated than the Greek Trinity, or Augustine's hermeneutics, simply adds frustration to a modern world in which everyone has come back except Spengler and Hegel, and I am thinking that they never really went away.

Under Vespasian's edicts the Christians cried, *"Nero redivivus!"* But there are beneficent rebirths too. Augustine rides in a thousand exhibits—Augustine's time in Bergson and Whitehead, his *Two Cities* in Hutchison and Maritain, his involvedness in Heidegger, his anthropology in any reformed realism and in the papers of the World Council of Churches. The third-century heresy about the "Father-sufferer" is at the bottom of any relevant modern soteriology. Unamuno recovers Kierkegaard and Marcus Aurelius. By a fluke of a wild auto wheel we are denied the maturing of the new bishop of Hippo, for the great North African, Albert Camus, was cut off just as he was climbing out of his Manichaean phase. Only Julian Huxley remains the same. Everything else changes, and most have gone the circle route which must make the shade of Oswald Spengler happy. Even for Toynbee, who restores Heraclitus, and Butterfield, who sees that all great revolutions turn in on their own middle, the parade is a cycle and we are bogged in the traffic at the square, milling and turning. The parade has lost its form and has become a wild and varicolored mélange. And even here a man keeps threshing about, lest he drown.

II

For the parade is no parade; it is a riot! Up and down in the sea of faces that was a parade but is now a maelstrom there dances the ghost of form that rested on Aristotle. There is no longer a beginning, middle, and end; no denouement, all edges blend, nothing cuts into new territory—no good, better, best; no cause, no order, no shape—but a mélange, a milling, pressured, gumming-up of the parade. In this, with all its sociological manifestations, we are involved. Here we must live our lives not as spectators, and the danger is no longer heresy. Here in this mélange, with both Athens and Jerusalem obscured, *some things simply never mattered less!* For the threat is not heresy, it is rather that we will choke on our exhaustion, pile up on the circle, and quit looking for a new cutting edge. Here, now, one begins to see, there never was an ordered parade with one exhibit following another. It has always been a *pot-au-feu* with all the condiments floating in the brew.

There is no longer form, it is the end of entity, so you pick up Faulkner's *The Sound and the Fury*, but you throw it down, startled, for this idiot, Benjamin, through whose mind there floats this hopeless disconcatenation of recollections, is no idiot at all—he is me! There is no beginning. One simply falls into a mass without edges. There is no time, no shape; Aristotle has become Freud. The unconscious rules. Form is dead. So you find, as Monsignor Knox puts it, that in heaven all are saints and in purgatory all are sinners, while in the church and on earth there are all sorts.

We find Hindu determinism in bed with reformed theologians, Catholic authoritarianism in Baptist conventions, Fascism in PTA chapters, German racism in junior colleges and so-called Christian pulpits, and that evil 1840 Southern theology appears again in South Africa's Reformed churches. You hear a jazz mass, sit in a Gothic movie house, find the spirit of Greece in cemeteries, Nirvana in funeral homes, see a swastika painted over the Star of David, are served pineapple juice mixed with tomato juice in Dallas, find a Mohammedan dial-a-prayer wheel in Protestant churches, and locate the best of primitive art in public restrooms.

The power of the figure stunned me. Amos Wilder points out that Faulkner's Quentin, on the day he became a suicide, broke the crystal on his grandfather's watch, then stripped its hands, as if he would stop time, but the formless, handless monster, with its useless blood-stained face, kept ticking out the drops of his life. In this *salto mortale* some things never mattered less. In a world that is eating out its innards in a revolution could there be a revelation? The agonized search for new symbols, for new meaning behind old symbols, continues, and this is our "sole common grief," our "common weeping." This is where a man comes "to eat the flesh of his own soul." Here reason becomes a matricide; love can die here. For if, after half a lifetime of searching, a man can spell the names of physicists, psychiatrists, theologians, and philosophers, but finds a home in neither Athens, Jerusalem, Vienna, nor Madison Avenue, may he not then be in position to find himself with no values at all except the personal? And is this the door to his redemption?

III

Is it possible that out of this kind of agon there could emerge a clear distillate? I am profoundly moved by the agony in which the church clings to its old frames in the face of this formlessness—this death of time. I am stricken dumb, between Sundays, at my own audacity; that in a shape like ours I would actually climb my stairs and call to passersby about God when I am but a befuddled man. Is there any future for this and for us? I do not know, but I have staked my life that the future lies with persons in a community of relation that can be discovered. On this I believe a man can rest his claim to be called a minister. Here I believe I can see an emerging hope that men can find some groves of trees in which to rest and work between their clawings at the abyss which threatens us with meaninglessness. The future, any future, has always lain with the personal.

This is the distillate coming out of an aching center. This is not something you have to swallow hard and believe. "In the beginning is relation." The only value we have is the personal in relation. This is the revelation, this is the center to which everything began years ago to point. Here we can come together in a community of inquiry and affection, for here it begins to appear that not only Jesus Christ but in some inverted and perverse fashion even Feuerbach, Freud, and Nietzsche are pointing to and seeking the personal in relation. An amazing hope has come to me of late. To this, Gilson, Marcel, and the Jesuit Teilhard de Chardin are all pointing. Camus had turned this way, preceded by Buber, Paul Tournier, and a holy, holy company.

When I tried to say these things once, my favorite sociologist called it "magnificently romantic." I answered in distress, "Doctor, do you mean magnificently preposterous?" For this is the surd, our hope lies in this absurd: the future lies with the presently insignificant; it rests in spirit and will, not with flesh and desire; with those who will hope and work, not with despair, or acquiescence in meaninglessness, or in the abomination of history. This is the surd: that the future should lie with Nels Ferré's love, which I saw once on a postcard from London to a man in trouble, more than it lies with his thought, which I have seen in books. This is the surd: that the future lies with the personal and the relation that can be recovered in the personal which is centered in that magnificent offer: "I, if I be lifted up from the earth, will draw all men unto me."

This is what it is all about. Strange, isn't it, that Jesus Christ should ache so to see the personal recovered? But if and as it is recovered, doctors will know how to tell their patients they must die, lawyers will become human, salesmen will lose their false faces, pastors will be able at last to forswear every vestige of the professional, and men will become men to each other, beholding "thy face as if it were the face of God" and we will see men like the man described in the Sermon on the Mount, but not by a mere ideal.

There is a work of redemption to be done, and this Jesus Christ means to us Christians. He will do this work; he has done it; he is doing it. God has come to meet us in relation. Love will do this thing, and at this point the things which never mattered less go away, the parade has its lusty noises stifled by distance, the traffic jam loses its frenetic pressure, we begin to hear voices, then one another, we recognize each other because redemption has come alive when persons in relation have begun to hear each other. And just here a man can become a minister of God, if he will.

Sénancour, in words dear to Unamuno, cried out: "Man is perishable. That may be so; but let us perish resisting, and, if it is nothingness that awaits us, do not let us so act that it will be a just fate." And this is the fantastic surd: that men may so resist the impersonal that death is absurd. Every man who has heard you can be maintained—in relation. And this is why we cannot let him come down from the cross where he has heard us—we dare not let him come down. If we should, there would be nothing left for us but to go out to his grave in the night and howl, for here is where he gives us what we have to sing about. Here relation becomes possible and makes a ministry a possibility.

I first began to suspect myself of being a professional twenty years ago when, clutching my brand-new ordination-gift prayer book, I held my first funeral for a man I did not know at Fort Knox. It was an agony to hear myself making those pre-prescribed holy noises, but I did not then know about the Cross, and one lifted up, and moments of relation, and what it is to hear a man as he dies, and to die with him if not for him. But I have tasted it now—and I decry and deny the former ignorance. A man can relate to men. He can become all men. He can be a redeemer—frocked or not. And in this redemption of relation he can live.

Through that Thou, I am becoming a person. And here a unique and unrepeatable event has happened. Here in a new incarnation, a whole kingdom of hope and potential has begun to be. This relation has its tensions, and this is suffering. It has its contradictions, and this is sin. It has its paradoxes, and thus it knows of death. But it has its interruptions in the form of new incarnations and its continuity which is eternal life, and in this person in relation a man can serve.

If this distillate is a new humanism, it seems inevitable, for it is all we have. Let it be, or let God be declaring us all null and void. Our hope is in the recovery of the person in relation. Nothing else matters—much. It is, I think, very unlikely that any of us will be theologians enough to help. There are good ones around and not many of us will qualify. But maybe we can be men enough—to help; so we go on with our work, seeking to become theological persons, knowing that our work begins and ends in relation between persons. There will be almost nothing we can do for or with our people except in terms of a discovered or a created or a given relation. If Savonarola himself were to preach from eight to four daily where I now serve, he would still be unable to do what that exciting church needs except in terms of relation.

So we go on with our work. It begins and ends in relation between you and them and us and them and God. And lest we be tempted to use our skills and our people and our advantage and our God, may we know early the shock of having to relate to men who have rejected us. If we can accept these and this, we will be able to accept the demands of the community of persons which grows within the "commonwealth of value." And thus we may taste the glory of the kingdom of God with such gladness that we can sing of it for our supper without ever being professionals or ashamed of more than our own sin.

Part I

The New Human Race
A Categorical Imperative

In the Valley of Achor, a sump of despair filled with storm-soaked and battered floats left over from the once festive parade of nineteenth-century theological fraternities, there is a milling and turning—but no parade anymore. World War II with its antecedents, and the threat of the war that will end war—and man—has set us to backing and filling over fields plowed with nuclear warheads and littered with the debris of modern peace plans. The parade fell off the high road into a low and soggy morass—it goes nowhere anymore. For an existentialist has no direction and no answers. He can have none and keep his rubric title. If he does not remain preoccupied with himself, in his situation, involved where he is, he no longer is an existentialist. He is a humanist, or a Christian, or an idealist—and everyone knows these roads lead nowhere.

But who, being human, can stay where he is? I propose to put two very old answers in combination—two very old roadbeds run together at last—to project a possible access road to a better and higher way—for now. Who knows? Perhaps it will lead to a *camino real,* a royal highway, for is there not somewhere from this slough to be found "a highway and a way"? Shall there not be a "highway for the remnant of his people, which shall be left from Assyria"?

I

The Prospect of a New Humanism

The Death of Classic Man

Otto Knille's lithograph entitled *Weimar 1803,* brings together, among others, Schiller, Niebuhr, Herder, Wieland, Schleiermacher, Hegel, and Fichte, in various attitudes of listening, waiting, attention, respect, around a central massive figure. But at center, really, is not the Greek statuary, it is the towering Johann Wolfgang von Goethe.

Huge of body, calf, thigh, and shoulder, massive in head and brow, with a gorgeous and arrogant pride, he dominates the assembly just as he did "his own time," for does not his century bear his name? Matthew Arnold called him "the clearest, largest, most helpful thinker of modern times." Schiller thought that of all the men he had known Goethe was of greatest worth. And Wieland, utterly carried away, said Goethe was "the greatest, best, most magnificent human being that God ever created."

Here is the Man, *Uomo universale,* every-compartment-full-man, the *göttlich.* He is poet, dramatist, novelist, critic,

27

botanist, physicist, zoologist, art collector, archaeologist, and court counselor. His own age called him "happy" in his birth, ancestry, and make-up; "happy" in his breeding, circumstances, position, destiny, and epoch. So happy, indeed, that one asks "How happy can you get?" In him the German mind comes into a "second summer," a new life, for the followers and imitators have made him a "two centuries man."

Eckermann, who called his nine-year diary *Words of Goethe,* followed like a child, and records that, even in death, at 83,

profound peace and security reigned in the features . . . the mighty brow . . . the divine magnificence of the limbs. The chest . . . powerful, broad, and arched; the arms and thighs . . . full and softly muscular; . . . nowhere . . . a trace of fat or leanness and decay. A perfect man . . . in great beauty.

Here indeed was classic man, giant man, competent hero, complete man. This, I say, is classic man, the best man the best culture of nineteen centuries could make. Here, sure enough, in heroic prototype, is the new human race!

Where did we fail? Why did not the new man come off well? What explains Goethe's inability to call more Goethes into being? Why is this giant so impotent? What explains our gross defection? There is such an abyss between Goethe and Hitler in less than a long lifetime. Albert Schweitzer's memorial to Goethe and Adolf Hitler's Reichstag power came within a twelve-month span. What gives rational, classic man such a hard time of it? Why does he no longer bloom well, and how is it that he comes off so poorly?

Is it just the gap between *knowing* and *doing?* Is this unhappy incapacity so simply explained as to be bounded by the fact, the most obvious fact of all our experience, that to *know* the right or best and to *do* the right and best are two quite different matters? Is there represented here some dread malady of Schopenhauer's will and Freud's id, which Thomas Mann finds so closely related?

How naïve that great Jefferson with his dreams of universal education! Resting on an incredible assumption of good will—that a man who knows right will *do* right—there was never a grander error! My brother writes, in our twenty-year continuing debate between research laboratory and presumptuous pulpit, that he is still committed to the proposition that "a man cannot think shoddily and act admirably"! Gross heresy! For, as a matter of fact, man very often *does* (think shoddily and act admirably). Indeed, he may act admirably without having thought at all! And even more frequently, and especially in these academic centers, does he not think well and do nothing? Think well in order to have to do nothing? Is it not common knowledge that if he thinks very clearly his courage for action dies; and if he acts very admirably, if he thought at all, it was hastily, shoddily put together out of images, myths, legends, analogies, and symbols his clearer thinking might have rejected? The rational man of the last century has a hard time of it! There is a great gulf between his knowing and his doing! He is estranged, split, halted, estopped—for something eats at his *will to do*. And hence we live our lives with the descent of the image! Goethe cannot redeem us. For modern, *ratio*nal man must use his ratio to spell and remember names like:

>Tarawa, Leyte, Tobruk, Lidice, Hamburg,
>Krakow, Hiroshima, PyongYang, Dienbienphu,
>Cuba, Congo, and Laos—all the day long.

And what medium, what witch of Endor, can call forth again the ghost of Goethe, of rational and classic man, in a world where all our media unite to declare his epoch-wide demise? He is hanged to the age-old gibbet—the bar between knowing and doing.

Here in our time and place we have to live amid the seeming triumph of the formless, the edgeless, and the hopeless. The new man as "Nude Descending a Staircase" is sexless, shapeless; a series of atonal sounds in decrescendo, light planes in a generally descending disorder. He lives his life and does what he does as political man, corporation man, research man, motivational man, anonymous man. He is stereotyped already by his mere presence at any vocational foundry until he joins by graduation the lemmings who rush en masse to fall into the whirlpool at the centers of power (misplaced), justice (denied), and love (debauched) that marks our modern urban culture as the depository for the faceless and vague.

And now the new fuzziness has crept even into religious art for children, as if nothing must be represented too clearly, too sharply, or *historically* at all. So cut loose are we from memory, mind, consciousness, and history that not only the Jesus of Nazareth but the donkey he rode into Egypt in his mother's arms has lost both form and face, and floats across the little children's storybooks like some mythical convenience put together by a committee.

This triumph of the faceless is no new thing. The descent of the image, the death of the *humanum,* the ultimate incredulity is no virgin-born newcomer, but it is perhaps the most serious threat we have ever known. This is no post-Christian era, but it *is* the twenty-fifth hour. Some modern theology *is* both denuded and atheistic. We *do* see the dying of our symbols, and Unamuno is right when he foretells "the shrinking of the universal."

There are other ways to slice this pie. Some have done it by making the American scene resemble a three-layer cake of frontier pietism (which won't quite die), nineteenth-century liberalism (which was never truly heard), and crisis theology (which our less critical crises allowed us to misunderstand). But all this does is comfort pietists, frustrate liberals, and turn systematic theologians into amateur psychologists.

Others set out bravely to "find" or "make" new symbols, never having learned that symbols find *the man*, not vice versa. Others deal with history as if it were some culprit we might catch, or focus on problems of language and meaning as if we were rational and could hear; but most of us are content to mouth some old heresy that has come back on stage and seized us.

By and large, the churches have reacted in one of three ways. Some ignore this twentieth-century agony. "Come weal or come woe, our status is quo." The professional spokesmen write their little diatribes against gambling, bundling, and bootlegging, and are generally in favor of Sunday observance, motherhood, free enterprise, and kindness to small animals.

Here and there the churches seem to have joined the whole complex in an attempt to get rich too, singing some version of the new beatitude: "Blessed are the sleek, for they shall never be rumpled."

And far more hopefully, still others—all too few—have begun to feel after the meanings we have missed. This search for meanings has begun to expose us to being grasped by other disciplines and other symbols. From our contemporaries in the study of persons, relations, societies, and structures; from psychologists, certain psychiatrists, sociologists, there begins to emerge a newer humanism which may yet be baptized by a new breed of personal theologians who are theological persons.

Meantime, in this flux that features the death of distinctives and the loss of will both to be and do, the hope that is left requires certain fundaments of us all. To this, and to these, modern churches will have to be committed. We are forced, are we not, to submit to the stripping of our vocabulary: to get relevant or be silent? We are forced to ask if there are biblical categories of meaning left to us that are useful. We are required to deal with, to make some disposition of, the extremes we face: the differences between a Goethe and a Hitler, a Francis of Assisi and a Richelieu. And finally, we are done unless we discover how one works and waits in a climate of despair.

The Continuing Temptation

Humanism is something of a nasty word in most good theological circles, and I have wished to be rid of it. It seems to smack too much of heresy and all that. I keep the word because the discussion must stay on earth; for we are men of "flesh and blood" who must die. Many other words have been ruined, too, and here is a term broad enough to hold both our confession and our obligation.

Humanism has always been my heresy. That some of my compeers have thought it stupid is no comfort to me. In those earliest reading years, consumed with history and its colors, such a complete sucker for the grand in all its forms, I had my heroes: Spartacus and Daniel Boone and the big slave in *Quo Vadis;* Stonewall Jackson, Germanicus, Richard the Lionhearted, Ulysses S. Grant, and the negro Pomp in *Cudjo's Cave;* Hugh Latimer, Attila the Hun—I've always had my heroes. There is a pattern to this inclination of mine.

During that long-ago first year of serious theological reading, how provoked I got with the smug-seeming delineations of God's attributes in the classic systematic theologies. How could even they be so sure about these things? Thomas Aquinas lived in a world apart. With what satisfaction, then, did a word from Immanuel Kant or David Hume answer for me the classical arguments about the existence of God? All those cosmological, ontological, and teleological arguments melted, prematurely enough, in a single afternoon, and only the anthropological argument seemed then to be worth a further investigation.

Why have I always felt such irritation on hearing pious phrases uttered by pious people in the face of inexplicable death, pain, misery, and poverty? Why do I keep excusing people for the sins they do that hurt themselves and not me? What is the utter fascination of minds like Feuerbach, Freud, and Nietzsche? Why did the social gospel and Walter Rauschenbusch have such an exhilarating effect upon me? Why was there such a zest for Jeremiah's revolts against the God he had to serve?

There is also in my pattern the little matters I have against God—If God is God, what about . . . ? Why do I always suspect the louder trinitarians of hiding from our true human situation by talking so much about God? There is a gorge that rises in my gullet at the bland familiarity with which many talk about God and their knowledge of him. On the other hand, there is this embarrassing ease in the presence of men who are doubters, hurters, and sinners. There is a loquacity which comes over me in talking to men about men and an embarrassing tongue-tiedness and discomfiture when I am expected to make too many noises in too sure a way about God. Why does Barth's "wholly other" appeal to me as little as it did when I first encountered it in Plotinus' incomprehensibility? Why did neo-orthodoxy speak mostly to me in terms of that brilliant and bloody doctrine of *man,* whose true situation demands his repentance but whose reconciliation with God demands and even waits on a reconciliation with men? Yet, if Barth's "wholly other" was so flatly foreign, why grasp at his recent *The Humanity of God* and the gorgeously written *Protestant Theology in the Nineteenth Century?* Why have I come so to love the man Barth though I am chilled by the Word hurled like a stone into the world? Why am I so disappointed when he cancels his brilliant insistence that God is Person by saying he is *the only one there is,* in spite of his ability to speak of the humanness of God as no other?

There are sections of the *Westminster Confession of Faith* and the first volume of Calvin's *Institutes* which cause a grave discomfort. John Baillie makes a seeker weep at his power to believe. Perhaps I do not believe in God but I do, I did, truly believe, the day Brunner's *Divine-Human Encounter* found me, and on the heels of this, Rudolph Otto's *The Idea of the Holy.* Why such a continuing regard for Max Otto and MacNeile Dixon? What is so attractive about the outrageous and the upstarty and the incorrigible in man? What is this utter fascination with the effrontery and temerity of Unamuno; what is the appeal of Don Quixote and the quixotic? What is this delight in biology and biologists who will talk of man's animal distinctives; and this fascination with the animalness of most men and the attraction of any human face?

Why does one feel such a compelling urge in ethics to begin in anthropology? Why does one seize so those texts that let him run on humanwise? What was that strange exaltation amidst which one had learned in Ephesians there is an aspect of his glory which God gets from us? Why was the youngster so relieved to discover agnosticism in the New Testament and the humanness in Psalms, Genesis, I and II Samuel and Kings, and Proverbs? What is this strange, mordant appeal of the book of Ecclesiastes, and what is the fascination now in the human relations underlying the Corinthian letters and Galatians? What is this exultation in the power of Paul's description of man left to himself in the book of Romans?

How can a man love both Luther and Erasmus? Why does he love Aquinas less than Augustine, the pre-Christian Augustine better than the new Christian Augustine, Pelagius better than the Bishop Augustine; and why does he love the sinner-confessing Augustine best of all? Why is he so devastated by some music and by some moments in worship? How can he feel such sensual joy in nature, sound, and color? Why does an irenic man who has every reason to be unpeaceful speak so challengingly, and what is this true *imago Dei* we have sought that has so prematurely convinced us that man is Somebody?

Is not all this to be explained by the fact that I am in love with man and mankind; that I see some basis for Feuerbach's contention that God is made in the image of man; that my preaching is filled with such anthropomorphic terms that I, too, run the risk of creating my God in the image of man I have loved? Is it not that I am a humanist and had best confess it? Is this embarrassment I have in claiming to know too much about God an honest rejection of temerity, or is it the background of a profound heresy with which I was inoculated in boyhood by men like Whitman, Voltaire, Clarence Darrow, H. L. Mencken, Sinclair Lewis, and the other iconoclasts who beat on my boyhood godhead until manhood became a substitute?

If so, it has left me ripe for a theology of incarnation; for what God who is God would not delight in the joy and the power and the thrust of man at his best forever and ever? From here, who can conceive of a higher joy than being man at his most and his best? This is a theology of identification. So now I find myself willing to talk about this. There's so little I can say for sure of God. Most of this has to do with a grace I have tasted from somewhere—mostly, indeed, from those I have loved and those who have loved me. This grace is of such sublime nature that it is the best evidence I have of the nature of that God who is God. And it is precisely through men in whom I have felt this grace that I have come to kneel, smitten, in the presence of God.

Is it strange that the door to God should open for a man through his love of men? Is there not something of a covenantal theology implicit even here? And are there not words other than humanism which we are in honor bound to recover—words like obedience, morality, hope, and expectation? Is it not entirely possible that in obedience to the demands of this grace one finds in mankind about him, a further door to the knowledge of God may open? So I can no longer say or even seriously intimate that I have difficulty believing in God. Nor could I say that my God is a man blown up to his ultimate dimensions. I can only say that I have always been humanistically rather than theologically oriented and that what distance I have come on the path to knowledge of God has involved a prior experience with persons.

This is why the charge made by Lutheran critics and friends of mine—that I am better at diagnosis than at therapy —is true. This I confess; and, I suppose, it will remain true as long as death comes up on me like it does and did yesterday. Riding across a field still glorious in its dying fall colors, I could see the spot where his horse stumbled at a gallop and fell, leaving the veteran rider neck-broken and limp, unable to see again, and feel, and taste, and anticipate the joys of the fields and the woods, the sky and the sun and the rain and the color, and the dark and the light. This business of death! If I had a better resurrection, I would not be so condemned to a continuing taint of humanism. At this door all our mere humanisms run out and we do not know.

A New and Chastened Man?

At this point you may well ask, what is meant by the use of this loaded term "humanism"? I am proposing a *tour de force* for a generation. I am proposing a discussion of faith in the active voice and the subjunctive mood; a way of life that acts on an "as-if"; a path to the knowledge of God that involves the ethic of act and a theology of person; and I am already too old to believe that what I propose is an innovation. I am suggesting, with Calvin, Baillie, Farmer, Temple, and others, that the path to knowledge of God is moral, and that by way of obedience a man can come to "see" and to "know." The word "obedience" is one in a litter of key words that have strewn our path as students since the late 1930's: words like "encounter," "response," "commitment." And before the new word, which now seems probably to be some form of the Anglo-Saxon term "help," looms across the theological horizon, we might do well to take seriously the word which is still with us, the word "obey." Obey what? The light we have and the God whose better knowledge by us may well indeed wait on our obedience.

Once, in answer to a query from a layman who had a speech to make, I tossed off one of those jackrabbit definitions which still remains in my backyard to haunt me. It hops and skips around in the night whenever I think of what I am expected to do and to be in the ministry. It went like this: "A seminary is a place where men come to learn what can be known of God and man and where they are committed to getting the two together." How presumptuous can one be! And now, a long, long way out of seminary; a veteran of most of the classic descriptions of God, doctrines of God, dogmas about God; a reader of books on revelation, inspiration, the Holy Spirit, the Trinity, the Incarnation, I confess that I long for God, have waited for God and Godot, have run after God, have said more about God than I know; have worshiped God, felt for God, listed God, analyzed God, prayed for God, to God, with God; and, like the rest of you, have beat on the gates of heaven when they were brass for some word from God to say. And on occasion I have been expected to speak to people about God with the acrid taste of my brassy words running through my nostrils as I spoke, realizing even in the act of speaking that I had sought every way of knowledge to God, even the mystic way of isolation, except the one way of finding him: the way of obedience. I have always had more light than I have been willing to follow, and so have you.

Baillie breaks through to me at this point when he says: "Little indeed do the Greeks and the Barbarians know of God and His Holy will, but they know enough to be far better men than they are." And so do I. It is time that we remembered that in this culture, in this time, in this place, it is thoroughly possible for us to realize that "not one of us has been left alone by God, that we have been sought out from the beginning, that from the beginning we have possessed more light than we have used and that this seems to be a necessary part of our confession of sin."

I am saying, let us rest, for now, the doctrine of God in its present state of development. Let us turn to the consciousness that we have used the doctrine of God to keep from having to face the facts of man and mankind. There is no point in our continued praying to the Almighty to save a world he has commissioned *us* to save. The strength is in our hands. The knowledge is in our minds. We lack only the will to be and to do, and for these we can pray. Those days, those rare days, in which I have been very sure of God have been those days when, for the moment at least, I was able to obey the light I already had received from God. I now know I can expect no new light until I have followed that which I have already received.

By humanism, then, I mean the willful, devoted, reverent turning away from preoccupation with knowledge we are not equipped to expand and the devoted acceptance of our place where we are, as we are, with the strength that is already in our hands, to be committed to the social, personal, redemptive, and prospectively revelatory tasks that confront us. What if there is no peace except the peace we make? What if there is no cleansing except the cleansing we do? What if God's redemption and God's purpose and God's coming and

God's kingdom are, insofar as their effective realization are concerned, truly in our hands? What if it is *unto us* that a Child has been born and a Son is given?

I propose acceptance on the part of Christian men that the making divine of the human may rest in the lap of our obedience.

II

The Necessary
Triumph of Grace

Premature Humanism

Here in America we are not finished
with the nineteenth century; and what is more, the nineteenth century has not finished with us. Indeed, few of us
know much about it. How pretentious we are! In the heaving
sea of historical theology, trying to survive that last three
weeks' squall of lectures covering modern Christianity, we
caught glimpses of Hegel, Kierkegaard, Ritschl, Troeltsch,
Harnack, and the main ideas of the German biblical scholars.
We were trained by men who had been trained in Schleier-
macherian traditions, but we neither knew nor could judge
the nineteenth century. We do not yet know the men who
made contemporary theology happen—the men behind
Barth, Tillich, Bultmann. Of those who will see this writing,
which of us really know Hölderlin, Rilke, Schelling, Heidegger, or the teachers at Berlin, Tübingen, and Halle who
lie behind Paul Tillich? Who knows Herder, Gogarten, the
Blumhardts, Thurneysen, and that obscure one, Kohlbrügge,
all of whom lie behind Barth's *Romerbrief?* Not even Over-

beck's critical word about the audacity of all who theologize has gotten across to us. We simply do not know the century that will not yet release us. Even when we come to American theology of the nineteenth century our memory is poor enough. Most of us began where we came in and are not aware of the chorus, offstage now, but which has still the lines that carry the play.

While nineteenth-century American liberalism did put an effective quietus on the theological respectability of seventeenth- and eighteenth-century Pietism, it is also true that nineteenth-century American liberalism was never able to consolidate its gains. The new world envisioned by our nineteenth-century liberals could not come off. This is true, in part, because they were not able to keep that which should have remained from the Reformation. Their fundamental loss was the doctrine of God. From this defection it seems to me every consequent weakness arises. But of this, more later. Notice now the prematurity of their humanism.

So premature was the humanism of nineteenth-century American liberals that we are not yet able to use the word without creating nervous reaction on the part of many modern theologians. It has taken an entire generation of "crisis" theology to create a base upon which we can now turn to the human and manward references derived from God in his relationships with mankind. The error of our nineteenth-century liberalism was its use of human powers, human obligations, human concepts, and human work to produce an "arrived-at" kingdom of God. The implicit error of our nineteenth-century liberalism lay in its idealism, but the problem with their idealism was not that it had a closed end, the kingdom of God; it was rather that it rested on an open bottom—no ground for beginning, just a continuity without base. God and the kingdom of God were values at which we would arrive, rather than sources from which we begin. Riding on the means of an evolutionary process at work in a world where things would automatically become better, with the kingdom of God as a goal at which we would in time arrive, and without an adequate doctrine of God or of man on which to stand, nineteenth-century liberals were truly children of their times.

Let me note some of the most effective limitations of this premature appeal to humanism:

First, the utilitarian theology. Is it a fair rule to say that "what is scientifically impossible shall not be laid as obligatory belief on the neck of modern man in the name of religion"? Is it possible to have "a kind of theological referendum, a democratic change in theology"? Is this not close to an ungodly *vox populi, vox Dei,* in which God is instructed by precinct vote of a majority? Is it possible to expand and readjust major sections of doctrinal theology to make room for religious convictions summed up in a new social gospel? Does this not make theology collapsible and expandable, even expendable, in the interest of an arrived-at line of thought?

Notice the extremely naïve view of human nature: "If the people were free they would stop exploitation," says Walter Rauschenbusch. So far, I am more impressed by Andy Brown's statement to Amos, "If the smart ones ever quit taking advantage of the stupid ones, it would upset the whole balance of stupidity." Can evil be regarded as a variable factor in the life of humanity, which it is our duty to diminish? Is it true that the worship of various gods and the use of idols is no longer one of our dangers? Is it true that the misuse of the holy name has lost much of its significance? Does not the view of human nature held by nineteenth-century liberals require the illusion that men could build a new society through education and moral suasion? Are not nineteenth-century liberals participants in bourgeois optimism? Did nineteenth-century liberals have a true understanding of the class struggle? Are not nineteenth-century liberals as a whole guilty of entertaining too high a view of man left to himself?

A further limitation appears in the equation of evil and sin. When corporate sin can be socialized into salvation by co-operative work, this means to the nineteenth-century liberal that evil is being replaced by salvation. Superpersonal evil in the nineteenth-century liberals is always superpersonal sin. This is too narrow a view. It does not recognize the evil that is not destroyed by redemption from sin. It does not consider the evil that is nonmoral or even beyond morals, as Nietzsche knew.

Our nineteenth-century liberals made history the matrix in which everything happens. This is a kind of humanistic naturalism rampant in the times. Their view of history was too institutional and never personal enough. Hence, nineteenth-century liberals placed too much blame and too much hope upon economic forces. The belief in progress by development is too pronounced. The shift from catastrophe to procession is too easy. The evolutionary optimism of these times required two great world wars to slow down.

Nor did our nineteenth-century liberals have a tool for the accomplishment of their social redemption. The church of the nineteenth-century liberals was a legitimate church in the dative case, but it was as barren as that of the left wing of the Reformation. Among nineteenth-century liberals no creative work was being done on the doctrine of the church so far as I can discover. The church is wholly identified with its institutional reflection (the Catholic error). There was no great church as God's channel of redemption in history (the sectarian error). The kingdom of God was the only entity beyond the institutional church. In the emphasis on the kingdom of God, nineteenth-century liberals lost the realm of redemption, the great church. This is the sectarian weakness most needy of correction in the councils of a world ecumenical movement.

The absence of church in the grand sense created a poverty of understanding about worship. Though a man like Rauschenbusch claims the church is a fellowship for worship, though he puts new language into liturgy, and though he prays like few saints have prayed—and with more effect than most—this same man marks off worship as "mass" too easily. There is no note like Temple's *conservatio mundi*. It was even insisted that the social gospel could give meaning to baptism and the Lord's Supper instead of seeing that the direct reverse is true. The church would be put to a pragmatic task and judged on its effectiveness in creating the kingdom of God. The church would be "used in socializing salvation." Paul's body of Christ is a socialized superman. The church displaces the Kingdom in a mechanical fashion. Just as it was with theology, the view of church is too utilitarian, and there is no high insistence on the communion native to reformed theology.

The limitation of our nineteenth-century liberals with respect to their view of the kingdom of God is primarily their loss of the past, past perfect, and historical present tenses. Their statements about the Kingdom "provide an Omega but lack an Alpha." They were speaking truly when they said the Kingdom is the supreme end; they did not know it as the point of departure. They did not see that it is more than something at which we arrive in time because it is also that within which we live and supremely that from which we came. This weakness rises in their doctrine of God and Kingdom which lost the *a priori*, the "given already," the "prior to our experience," as well as after it. They did not see the Kingdom as the *total creative redemptive effect of God in the universe.* The kingdom of God is not "humanity organized according to the will of God." This is partial, too narrow and exclusive. The kingdom of God is God, three in one, with angels, archangels, principalities and powers, universes, creations, redemptions, and consummations, over all of which

45

God rules. Truly the Kingdom is the supreme end, but it is also the point of departure. Properly, the nineteenth-century liberals said the kingdom of God was the marrow of the gospel. The doctrine of the Kingdom does require the social gospel, for otherwise the redemption of the whole world is just an annexed scheme. But if this be true, the doctrine of God's kingdom must be an adequate statement of that doctrine. Whence comes the Kingdom? Who truly builds it? Can Jesus of history be said to be its initiator? There must be past tense to Kingdom.

The notion of the arrival of the Kingdom indicates also a faulty eschatology, for "arrival" is not "coming." Implied also is that humanism which builds this Kingdom. Luther escapes this in the phrase, "The Word must do this thing and not us poor sinners." Anything less that still has hope is a sort of happy humanism; *in extremis* it longs for an earthly Eldorado; and so does Karl Marx.

Liberal views of atonement have much that can be useful today in our new attempt to dredge up values within a redeemed humanism. For example, the death of Christ is the demonstration of the power of sin in humanity; the Cross does make any easy treatment of sin impossible. The Cross is the supreme revelation of love; Jesus does bear our sins by way of racial solidarity; his death does affect God as a new beginning. Here men do "watch sin go full-length and love go all-out." But the salvation of superpersonal forces is surely more complex than this. Salvation is not by demonstration; it is rather by identification. The death of autocracy is not salvation, and democracy is not a kingdom. To be poverty-stricken is not to be redeemed; nor is the meagerness of the ministry a true badge of humility. Nineteenth-century liberals seemed to lack any real encounter; they have no true Christ in history; no proper identification with much less *union* with Christ. Do they assume this, or that this has been said? Then why does Richard Niebuhr see in Walter Rauschenbusch the victory that comes "not by grace but by merit, no suffering of the son of God nor forgiveness for the sinful society"?

And this is the heart of the matter: God is no very great bother to the nineteenth-century liberals. The holy God who is very, very near they seemed to know well; the holy God who is very far away was not a real problem. The first table of the Ten Commandments seems to have gone away; the new idols are no threat to the God who is immanent. How close are these nineteenth-century liberals to Feuerbach when it is said that

God is not only the spiritual representative of humanity; he is identified with it. . . . In us he lives and moves, though his being transcends ours. . . . He is the life and light in every man. . . . A spiritual commonwealth with God in the midst of us. We must democratize the conception of God. . . . [Jesus] democratized the conception of God. . . . He not only saved humanity; he saved God.

If nineteenth-century liberals had no truly transcendent God, this is the key to their premature humanism; for without God transcendent the dogmas of history, eschatology, church, kingdom, and atonement are radically affected.

All our nineteenth-century theological limitations stem from two serious bypasses in the times and in their development. The transcendence of God is no real problem. The true make-up of personality is not understood. Without proper understanding of the depths of involvement in evil of every individual, the expected triumph of the kingdom of God as a social enterprise is an incredible naïveté. Without God transcendent, no community is possible and Kingdom, church, and history lose all depth dimension within a flat world that knows no "edge of the times."

This is why nineteenth-century liberalism could not pull

off its victory over the seventeenth- and eighteenth-century Pietism. It stood in a morass; it had no *a priori;* its humanism rose, like any other evolutionary humanism, from the swamps of antiquity. Indeed, may this not be the key to the whole? The nineteenth-century liberals were unable to come to grips with God creator, *creator ex nihilo;* even the possibility of such faded before the new physics, the new universe, the new glorification of man. The times indeed awaited a mighty correction.

A Mighty Correction

Wait for the God who is God! God is! And the audacity of the cry about *totaliter aliter* sent sympathetic vibrations rumbling along the girders of European theology. The whole structure became a vibrant, matching, open diapason coupled in octave by synthetic pitch to the original cry. That first Mozartian woodwind created such a rumbling response from the great pipe that those who could not reach the pitch crossed seas to join themselves to other organs. For forty years the pitch has held with the variations that time and temperature produce in any great-voiced organ.

How sad to see that first audacious countercry absorbed in the orchestration! How fervently one hopes that an aging Karl Barth will not overcorrect the audacity of the day he "first stood up" against his "great teacher Harnack." Let him remain near the stance he took that first day; let lesser lights do the hyphenated rearranging of the original score that time seems always to require. How sad if he should go full circle and disappear in the score from which he first ejaculated that note to change the whole oratorio.

In his recording of Handel's *Messiah,* Sir Thomas Beecham drives orchestra and chorus into quadrupled tempo at the close of part two, and the "Hallelujahs" become a fantastic, shattering speaking in tongues, a mighty unsayable glossolalia. Let Barth stay here where we can hear him. But he will not. He is already off on the return to his old anathema, Schleiermacher, where we came in, but who can temporize about the mighty correction we have taken. Lesser organs in far-distant chapels practice the holding of the pitch he used to set the Western world to hearing.

It has followed that at every point in systematic theology radical correction of nineteenth-century weaknesses has been experienced in our generation. This is true especially with respect to the doctrine of God and the doctrine of revelation. (God reveals *himself,* not propositions—this is the death of fundamentalistic theology when understood.) For it opens the door on that understanding that all theological propositions are of human origin and are cast in human frames of reference. It forces every "sacred list" of "fundamental" assertions to submit to the prospect of correction and brings inspiration into the halls and corridors of this present time, refusing to abandon it to the time when God was speaking only Hebrew or Greek. The doctrine of the Word of God as continuing in the Christ in this present time opens the door to vast new hearings and obeyings and puts at our door the right to expect him to speak in very human contexts. This radically alters the shape of every dogma that depends upon a hearing of the Word.

The doctrine of man now features a radical reconstitution of reformed realism through which realistic views of sin, evil, politics, and society are being recovered. The doctrines of sin, salvation, church, and history, though marked with a continuing and radical disagreement among men in the same general school of thought, rest on the recovery by biblical theology of the idea of God in history, active in our times and in us. This means that it is now possible to talk again in terms of faith in the active voice. The demand of the gospel of God upon mankind, along with the human powers and potential that lie within our grasp, constitute both arms of the life of obedience. This life becomes a possibility and a means to new light about both God and ourselves.

On this platform of nineteenth-century liberalism's permanent contributions, as corrected by crisis theology, a new humanism, *implicit in the gospel from the beginning,* can now be understood. This is a new cutting edge for contemporary theology. It will require the undertaking of a new conversation between Reformed and Arminian thinkers, between Jonathan Edwards and Isaac Watts.

Christians are legion now who believe that new light has come and is coming into a world that has barely begun to understand itself. We know the folly that claims to know all that we need to know. We believe, too, that truth has already been granted which men ignore or neglect at their peril. We relate this truth to that God who is beyond and within history; who reveals himself, not propositions, in the face of Jesus who is the Christ; whose unavoidable Cross involves those identified with him by faith in a life of corporate responsibility for corporate sins; in which moral fiber reveals its presence in our identification of ourselves with a brotherhood of believers which no longer seeks to separate itself from the common life and agony of all mankind; but follows the holy presence of Christ in worship and work of God in Christ; with whom we are called to participate and whom we meet at the center of things in our worship and at the edge of things and time in our needs.

This is a world theology. We learn from all who can teach us, the host who seek the light we seek. And we learn, too, from the disciplines of history, literature, art, philosophy, biochemistry, mathematics, physics, and experience. It is even possible for us now to confess that we have taken our cosmology from physics, our teleology from chemistry, and more importantly to us, we wait on depth psychology to show us more of the morphology of that self which has always stood in such a desperate need of redemption. Other disciplines force us to face those super-selves in society, the power structures apart from which we cannot live, and which stand in need of the same redemption.

On this theology, with human powers but recently discovered by us to be within ourselves, we believe ourselves ready to begin to face the reality of the new human race, and we believe we can see the emerging face of that man, the man in Christ, who not only is constitutive of the new humanity but is constitutive of the new church that must result from the proper facing of ourselves and our potentials as persons.

But spare us the nineteenth-century crime of beginning as if there were no God! And here the demand of the time is grievous, for who can go beyond "God beyond God"—who can think of "wholly other"—who can live with a God "not factual"?

We shall have to be more audacious than this in our theologizing. We shall have to strip back to our beginning and become less sophisticated than these carry-overs from Plotinus and his incomprehensibility. We shall, as persons, have to use the power of persons. This means we shall have to speak in terms that are anthropomorphic. *We shall have to use a symbol as if it were so, and talk of God as Person.*

And of what are we afraid in being anthropomorphic? Do we fear we shall be "dogmatizing the provisional"? Who has not, if he dogmatizes at all. This is Overbeck's "audacity." How can we escape being anthropomorphic? We are men and not God. Shall we dogmatize a mystery? Xenophanes did, and called it *Nous;* but his progeny have produced what Luther called "reason, the great whore"—meaning that our rational powers will serve any master, even atheism and nihilism.

God of Grace—God as Person

There is something utterly audacious in speaking of God as Person, yet it is a thoroughly biblical point of view. The primary agony is to escape the *implication of need* that goes with our understanding of what it is to be person. But what if one cannot really escape implying need to God?

This implication of need. Karl Barth consistently refuses to make; yet I find in Karl Barth a bridge that seems to require the reference to God as Person, although Barth himself will not do this very happily. In spite of his difficult sections on God as Person, Barth does not like this kind of talk. He cannot afford to like it; it gets in his way. He does not have to use it; his use of it is an accommodation to moderns. Nothing is to be gained by calling God Person or by refusing to say "person." The important thing is to say that God is the One who loves.

Very well, let us say "love" and not "person"—and what has been said? One tires elsewhere of the endless semi-sophisticate use of so many Greek words for the English word "love." Do they nowhere come together as having issued from a common base? Were Rothe and Lotze so far wrong as to be dismissed by two handsful of Barth's very smallest type when they claim that God is not to be denied "everything that constitutes the peculiar excellencies of human nature" or that no other form than personhood could "satisfy the soul-longing to grasp the highest"? What about this love business? Or better, first, what about the person?

Somewhere in his thousands of pages Barth says, perhaps more than once, "It is because man is fallen, not because he is finite, that man is incapable of God." If the barrier to God is truly my sin and not my finiteness; if the Divine truly participates, as Barth shows, both as transcendent and immanent, and if Barth, as he does, truly evades immanentism and pantheism, is it not clear that the only way God can participate in the finite and the infinite is in terms of personhood? Grant that "one does not say God when he speaks of man in a loud voice." Grant Kierkegaard's "infinite qualitative difference." Be willing, in some modest way, to speak in terms of "wholly other." Recognize the partial rightness of Barth's claim that "God is in heaven, you are on earth." There is still to be interposed against this the concept of the God who acts—and most magnificently, the God who comes. If reconciliation means, as Barth says, a "change of parts" between God and man, and if the barrier is sin which can be forgiven, not finitude which cannot be invaded; if God can truly come, and if he has truly come, the highest meaning of Barth's new revelation is just this: that what the nineteenth-century humanists grasped after—to get God to be Person—this was there all the time.

But Barth does not like this language. He gives to Rothe, Lotze, *et al.*, common ground with all who deny the personality of God. He says we say that "God is to be understood as the content of the highest human values." *Nein!* We do not so say! The quarrel is not as to whether this is a definition and a containment, not whether this is *all* of God, as if we take him in chunks; we know we have not described God when we say God. We do not say, with Feuerbach, that God is man. But we do say that this is all we can take in from who and where we are; that the God beyond God defies our further description; that to say more than "Person" is to talk nonsense; and that our highest values do participate in a characterization of God which, if seen from *there* rather than from where we are, would be seen to have been correlative with his nature, even if on terms of an infinitely lower denominator; and that we are justified, even compelled, to use only the language we have as limited by our highest experience of ultimates and no more than that language. Nobody *knows* fifteen hundred pages about God, even in German.

We do not deny that from here our view is a projection of our highest and best. We know it is that; but we insist on a subjunctive of faith, an "as if" that rests on a projection that strikes something in which our projection participates.

God is—we confess; but any predicate added must be said by us in terms of our ceiling. That is, the highest terms we have—those of personhood—apply. This means that we turn away from an Absolute we cannot think anyhow, or describe with the word "person," to a relative personhood which does participate in what we project the Absolute to involve if we could think it.

Lotze, Rothe, *et al.*, tried to carry the Absolute forward as a term and reconcile "person" with it. The agony is irreconcilable. We cannot do this. The contradiction between Absolute and Person (as being impossible of infinity) can be resolved only by staying with the term we can know (personhood) and postponing the use of terminology we cannot bear up under. In this sense Feuerbach is right when he says that *our theology is anthropology*. No doctrine of revelation gives us God's glasses—we have to use human terms or deny the necessity of the Incarnation. More than anthropological concepts we cannot use. Any reception is on our wavelength, and any broadcasting is limited to our band of sensitivity. Barth refutes Lotze, *et al.*, with the concept of *technical impossibility;* but the impossibility applies to carrying both Absolute and Person as terms. We choose Person; for the impossibility is with respect to the more than personal, not with respect to the less than Absolute. We know that God is more than we know; but we also know what we can know as participating in the "more than person" and use that to say "person at least," i.e., loving Father. More than this we cannot say short of arrogant supposititiousness.

Barth has said that the need of man does not make God's self-revelation inevitable—then what does? Is it a need in God to be known by man? And is this meeting, this encounter, this need in man met by corresponding need in God—is this the basis for covenant, reconciliation, the spoken, acted, done, Word in the first place?

Some sort of an approach like this has been evaded by almost everyone who has the temerity to speak of God as Person. The violation is not a violation of finitude. Nor is it an absurd humanistic assault on transcendence and infinity. It is rather that there is a given invasion of the finite by the holy One who in coming to us has become Person with all that implies of need and desire for our salvation. We do not postulate an absolute personality. We only say personhood participates, is truly symbolic of, the Absolute. We do not say "comprehensive personality"; we say relative person as the highest we can see.

This we have to say in order to say God loves. I do not hear Barth when he says, "Everything depends on the statement that God is the One who loves. But nothing at all depends on the statement that he is or has personality." To be able to love is constitutive of personality. How can we "do without it so long as what is intended in it is assured and accepted"? How is it that "nothing is to be gained by this concept and nothing lost" if only we say God loves? Have we not given up the ground of love in order to keep the wholly other?

But Barth has his own solution. God is the only Person there is! And what has *this* discovered to us. It ruins everything!

Is there, indeed and in fact, even in God, such a thing as *unconditioned* love? I can no longer accept Nygren's classic distinction between agape and eros. Does agape so far transcend our notions of love that it does not participate in the primary ground out of which all love rises? By unconditioned love must we mean so different a love from the love we can know that it becomes something other than the love we can know?

There is a sense in which love is unconditioned by the condition of the loved one. There is a sense in which love asks no questions, makes no demands, institutes no reforms. Paul is quite clear about this in the thirteenth chapter of I Corinthians where he says love is no reformer. This unconditionedness of love is with respect to the object of love; must it also maintain with respect to the love itself? It was "while we were yet sinners" that Christ died for us ungodly. The unconditionedness applies to the object of his affection; but if this applies to the affection itself as love, another word than love is needed, for love always rises out of need. Indeed, there seems to me no other ground for love.

I hear Karl Barth warn me not to try to bring love to a common ground, not to do this inversion, lest Deity be emptied of meaning. But is the answer to dichotomize so that I empty love of meaning? Then why use the word "love" with respect to God? Nothing is at stake as damage to God if I mis-theologize on God—he is God—but something is at stake if I empty love of meaning. Love has to mean love or be something other than love. And love still rises in need. Barth calls the language of E. Bohl "suspect when applied to God," but here it is: Love is "the inclination, the aspiration, the desire of our essence for another, the procession of a personality from itself, with the desire to go over to another or to take up the other in itself. . . . It cannot be alone, but it desires its like." If God cannot, because of his *aseity*, do this, he cannot love. If he can, his love participates in the ground of love —need and desire.

Love, says Paul Tillich, is "the drive towards the unity of the separated. Reunion presupposes separation of that which belongs essentially together." When Christ says, "With desire I have desired to eat this passover with you," it is but a reflection of the desire with which God has desired the salvation of sinners. Must not love live amidst both need and desire, or be something other than love? According to Turgenev, who knew the hungers, any total claim to love rests on a *craving* to be known and loved, loved *because* known, or loved *although* known. This means we are as audacious as we can be when we so glibly say God is love. It ought to be said less, and with fear and trembling.

Why do so many decent theologians still refuse to say that God needs us? Does it cut across God's majesty, his glory, his otherness? I watched Paul Tillich shy away from this in a public conversation with Gustav Weigel at Harvard. In *The Humanity of God* Barth says everything else, but refuses to say this word of need. Is it a greater heresy than Patripassianism to say that the Father needs? Is it a grander heresy than the Father as sufferer to say that the Father needs that which he has fathered? Does need in God cut deeper into his glory than suffering in God? Or does it follow from God's suffering that he should be also a needing God? Is it indeed the explanation of his suffering that he also participates in our need?

When Barth says God does not *need* his own being in order to be who he is, it is because God already *has* his own being. Is a need satisfied no longer a need? Is that which constitutes satisfaction of a need not necessary to the preservation of a satisfaction? The continuing satisfies the continually met need. The need remains.

Especially is it so that God's need of his own being is not threatened by our incompleteness. But God's need of our completeness does not minister to his own being; it ministers to his satisfaction, his glory, his communion with his creatures.

I do not quarrel with God's *aseity* (his self-derived being) —I only say he *needs* it, whether he has it or not, and he needs *us* for the completion of his satisfaction. *That* at least, waits on us, or we have no being. Love satisfied is no longer love—it is satiety. This is love—the not yet satiated—the never yet satisfied—the not yet enough—the need that needs.

This brings up the larger question of the true bond between God and man. Thomas Mann says that religion essentially implies a bond. In Genesis there begins this covenant between God and man. In *Joseph and His Brothers* one sees, not just an oriental esoteric notion of the relation of God and men, but rather the idea that God is somehow to get his constituency in man. That is to say, there is a mystical humanism which goes so far as to say that God is not God without man. One finds it in the West in Silesius: "I know that without me God cannot live a moment; if I am destroyed He must give up the ghost." Karl Jung focuses a perception he sees common to Schopenhauer and Freud at this point: "The giver of all given conditions resides in ourselves." Commenting here, Thomas Mann says, "Man's animal nature strives against seeing himself as the maker of his own conditions." Eastern minds have always been closer to this power to see the gods as given in the soul. Although Eastern thought distinguishes between subject and object, and refuses to have subject and object coincide, or refuses to make one proceed from the other, in the West only true European mystics can do this. In general, the notion that the soul is the giver of the given is intolerable in the West. It represents a *psychological* conception of God. It denies the rational concept of God. It is a *rabies theologorum* in the East, not West. Schleiermacher and Barth psychologize, but not on God! In the West, to say that God is bound up with the soul is equivalent to abandoning God. Perhaps this is why Barth cannot say that God needs us. To him it would be to fall away from the very concept of God.

In any case, the notion of the bond between the unholiness of man and the holiness of God implies one part being most intimately bound up with the other. Wherefore else, one should ask, would there be any bond at all?

It is in this sense that Abram is the father of God. Abram fathers God in that he perceives God and brings him forth. God's mighty qualities, described and ascribed to him by Abram, were God's own original possession. Abram does not invent them, yet in a sense he is, by virtue of his recognizing them and therewith by taking thought of them, making them real. God's qualities are indeed something outside us, exterior to Abram; but at the same time this perception and these qualities are in him and of the man as well. The power of one's own soul is at moments scarcely to be separated from these concepts. We are consciously interpenetrated and fused with them, and such is the origin of the bond which the Lord strikes with Abram as the explicit confirmation of an inward fact. The covenant is in the interest of both. Thomas Mann, in *Freud and the Future,* says that, "Need human and need divine here entwine until it is hard to say whether it was the human or the divine that took the initiative."

This is a shocking and heretical come-about, but it demonstrates what it means to think of God as Person. By what right we do this, philosophically and actually, is now demanding demonstration. The categorical imperative is that we think relatively and personally of everything, because this is the only way we can think or talk or know. We run this risk. Who can know an Absolute?

III

The New Human Race

Nineteenth-century theologians lost both man and God when they took their field and ground of operation "from the Gentiles." That is to say, theologians seemed to think of themselves as philosophers who needed to define their anthropological concerns against a backdrop and upon a ground acceptable to nineteenth-century thought. They seem to have assumed that there was no biblical ground upon which their structures could rest. Hence, they supplied a ground from current timber, they adopted an anthropology of the times which issued in, as Samuel Beckett demonstrates, the death of God in their century, and the funeral of man in ours.

A Prior Ground

Did we not fall into the same sump that trapped their energies? Have we not neglected and despised a fundamental base which has lain there almost too available all the while?

Is it not a gross mistake to allow a poetic, symbolic, noncritical, and inadequate world view, which does indeed enshroud the heavens and the earth for biblical writers, to keep us from seeing the one given biblical ground upon which we can stand and see a real hope? Is it not a gross heresy to allow biblical inadequacies in geography to destroy for us biblical competency, even indispensability, in terms of an adequate metaphysic?

The Holy Scriptures have not yet had an adequate anthropological reading. That is, a reading from where we stand as men. They were written by anthropoids, for us anthropoids of a higher order—why not read Holy Scripture anthropologically? We have too long read only theologically—and the ground upon which theological structures rise can be surveyed from here only anthropologically. Only God can read theologically! For this kind of reading too high a set of assumptions is demanded for us and from here. Have we not attempted to read writing we do not yet know how to read? It is our common failure—to seek to wear God's spectacles.

Let us begin to read at our own level; let us give the relative the priority it must have from here (Hartshorne). Let us see what men of Holy Scripture know about man before we come back to what is propositioned about God. Let us see if there is not an anthropological ground; let us see if all our structured ideas of God do not rise from an *a priori,* a categorical imperative already implicit in the experience of biblical man with men! For back of scriptural man's propositions about God are some assumptions about God he could have arrived at only through what he knew about himself, even by revelation. Not even God can speak to man without a grammar.

All this is not to define man's ground of being as man. Not at all! It is simply to say that the only kind of knowledge of anything we may have is relative and anthropological, for we are men and not God. It is to say that especially our structured knowledge (so-called) of God is derivative from our experiences with one another. It is to say that all revelation reaches us in human terms and through human experiences. But this is not to say that God is derived—not yet at least!

Nor is this to say that God was not prior for biblical man. *It is to say biblical man's knowledge of God is not entirely apart from his experience with man!* Biblical man knew God as the only source of existence, of his own experiences with nature, himself, and his fellows. He learned that God is given, prior, that God had given—but his coming to this was *posteriori*—not *a priori*. He learns how to think of absolutes by projection from the relative, not vice versa. We have been trying to know God as God knows God, and we have no strength for the task so long as all our experience is with relatives. We have to project from the relative of our experience, and even revelation is in terms we can understand. It comes through human terms.

The primal ground upon which all thinking rests, where it begins, is in man's ability to categorize. He can see that this is this and that is that. He can see differences and similarities. He can classify. This is the beginning of thinking. Theologizing is thinking. It begins where thinking begins with the addition of the awareness of *degrees* of difference between classes. Philosophy and theology begin in his powers of comparison. His sense of the Absolute is not given; it is gotten. He can see that this is more pleasing or better or prettier or tastier than that. He learns to think good for me, bad for me, I like, I like not, and from thence he learns to say bad, more bad, most bad, or good, more good, most good. Only then can he think all good. Of course all good was prior; but not in his experience. His powers to theologize about God began in his powers of comparison.

What is the ground, the primal ground, upon which a

theological structure can rise? Does it not begin in an observed fact of all human experience—that some men are so much better than others as to form classes of goodness?

From the beginning of moral life the path to knowledge of God has been moral. This is all I am claiming. But the ground from which we observe is the apparency of the moral in man—not God. Men do not have to remain as they are. Some are different. The moment we ask the *how* and *why* of this we approach a doctrine of God—but the *a priori* from the point of view of experience is that man has this potential —he can be better than he is. From here, any statement of God's nature is one that requires an assumption—but on this ground—the anthropological ground—we stand in experience. Our assumptions follow to explain that other, that mystery we encountered previous to our thinking, that numinous we were aware of premorality and by whose powers it came to be. The rational moral makes some sense out of the mystery we met prerationality and premorality. The *Mysterium Tremendum* is prebiblical. Biblical man is already there when he talks of his origins in Genesis. He is already in possession of the knowledge that rises from his observable, knowable relations with a new kind of man.

There is then a biblical metaphysic—a categorical imperative—which rises from the fact in experience of the observable, knowable relationships of a new kind of man. This is the ground of our theology from the manward view: the biblical anthropology knows about a different sort of man— the new human race. It is an indisputable fact of our experience. Its explanation requires a doctrine of God, a head of the race in terms of a pre-existent Son, a redemption, atonement; but these are doctrines derived from, given, after the apperception of that which is prior in our experience: to wit, the new race of men. The biblical man is always heading to this, and proceeding from it. He lives in this prospect, which is what it is to live humanly before God. One does not have to die as he is; he has moral prospects.

The Irreducible Remnant

This new kind of man is already in view when the Lord God walks in the garden in the cool of the day. He, the new man, is the prospect and the reality which biblical thought has even the great God seeking, coming to meet. Indeed this is the only God there is in the Bible—that God who comes to meet the man who came from God! Let us begin with this man who came from God. Perhaps we can hear more of the God who made him, sends him, and calls him. This is Christian humanism.

What, asks Karl Barth, is the obviously outstanding feature of world history? "It is the all-conquering monotony—the monotony of the pride in which man has obviously always lived to his own detriment and that of his neighbor." Take this feature, the fact of this dread monotony, and out of this, and its converse, recognize a biblical category that will do, that is prior, that is universal, that is true wherever man is man in all time. Adam was always like this, monotonously proud, except where he became no longer Adam. For this he has potential!

Admit it! Our reading of many biblical categories is dead. But for me at least this one is left: the category of the new humanity. The class is prior to the specimen. The existence of the class, a new human race, creates the awe-filled potential that we who are Adam do not have to remain as we are! Adam can become another. All growth is in it. This is how we make it on our journey—the hope that we do not have to remain as we are.

The Hope That Is Before Us

Adam—the old man—is here; and of the accuracy of his portrait we have 3,800 years of evidence; indeed, now we have ten thousand years of new evidence that Adam was always like this. But Adam, the old man, is head of nothing. He is not primal, nor progenitor; he is just early man, man-wherever-you-choose-to-begin, prebiblical man in the day he discovers his prospects and becomes biblical man. He is man on the threshold of manhood and is the head of nothing.

Biblical man lives prospectively for a long time before he sees the Head of the race. Heads do not appear at the edge of thresholds. They are a long-awaited end and appear midstage in the center of dramas. In most plays some manservant is on stage long before the master appears. The chorus does the prologues in Greek plays and Hamlet does not introduce his own appearing; there are always lesser lights. Johns who are baptizers and forerunners always precede Messiahs.

In the opening of the great drama God is onstage alone, and this seems appropriate enough, except that this introduction is a contrived introduction arrived at retrospectively and added as a theologization of a situation being explained after the event, for none of us was there to observe. The play begins with a lesser light, Adam, and the Head was yet to appear.

Biblical man is aware, long before the Coming, that his Head has not yet appeared, but he longs for him, strains after him, and always is man who participates in that from which he came (Adam) and that manhood to which he is called (Christ).

Everywhere one sees biblical man, he is in this tension between his oldness and his newness, and Christ, the New Man, the Only Man, is the face of the man that can emerge, the man who can *be* precisely because he cannot stay as he is. Biblical man is always Adam and Christ and somewhere in between. His calling is to the new humanity. The new humanity requires a new humanism. It cries out (with Feuerbach) that even God get human! Within this aged categorical imperative, the tension between the old man and the new Man, is it not possible for us to talk, and wait, and hope, and *do?* The emerging Christian humanism rests on it. The cosmic face of man has only seemed to be Adam—it is Christ! For God is very human too! He became like us! The Ultimate is concrete! Here the old liberals (never heard) and the fundamentalists (never very human) and psychological inquiry (now respectable) and theologians (becoming persons) can meet, and talk, and hear, and be changed! If only we do not keep tripping on the lip of some old ego.

And the extremes we face—the tensions and mighty contradictions we endure because we are all still between Adam and Christ? Can we not refuse to be part of the problem? As churchmen, can we not strip each other of sham, pretense, professionalism; confess our humanity and thus join the answer, not the problem? Can we not refuse this dread concrescence in which we keep settling, remaining open to new light, remaining fluid to effect the death of our provincialisms? Can we not refuse the admission that we have arrived? And do we not have now the power to clean some things as we go? Are we not able to *make* some justice and *do* some mercy and throw off pretense? Does not our own half-redeemed vision permit us such a sight of ourselves that we could begin to reject the mighty sin of misrepresentation? For if our true distinctive rests in our powers of communication, does not our basic guilt rest in our habitual *mis*communication? To this it is past the time to address ourselves, for it is the beginning of wholeness and the road to person in relation.

And how does one wait in a climate of despair? In this inter-biblical time, this transition from sense-filled to idea-possessed, this agonizing wait for the new image, the new light, the new idea, how does one wait and work?

He comes to recognize that any new has always been present in the old long before it was seen to be new. There are no sudden breaks. All our messiahs have been anticipated and longed for. The new is never really startling since it is already present. Therefore, one must work with the tools he has, with the comrades he has, where he is, for the "night which cometh" will find him less than God, in any event; but it need not find him less than man who came from God, nor unrelated to that God who would be man.

Part II

The Emerging Face
A Twentieth-Century
Extension

God truly waits for us in things,
unless indeed He comes to meet us.
—TEILHARD DE CHARDIN

The Face on the Bible Belt Wall

In that Protestant Eldorado where I live, most everyone
is so deeply wrapped in the mask and trappings of moralistic
pietism that few can conceive what else Christianity might be
unless it is the picture on our wall: Grandfather, in long
coat and striped trousers, mustachioed, vested, chained, keyed,
and caned, with hat in hand, coming down the stairs on Sunday, en route to First Presbyterian (ruling elder), hard by
First National (president), with Sons of Confederacy Hall
upstairs (chaplain and historian), past the local orphanage
(chief benefactor). That the picture not only has faded, but
never was Grandpa—or Christianity, either—never enters
most minds.

By and large, we have done well with what Grandfather
would have taken with him on to glory if he could. In the

main, we join more clubs, are generally more jaded and less pious, but we are just as certain of status with the Almighty and as sure of a resurrection in spite of the boredom of this present human existence, and we live by the image of this man on the Bible Belt wall. Whoever he was, he was not the new man for whom the world has waited. And though his foreign missions in China and the Congo are lost in ruins and his world has undergone at least three shattering revolutions, we carry on, for Grandfather thought he was the new man, and so do we—oblivious to what nineteenth-century liberalism did to pietism elsewhere.

To this day, pietism reflects itself in the existence of aged institutions of real philanthropy, built and given by men who very much wished to fulfill the Christian ethic. Pietists placed great emphasis on the "spiritual life"; they shared an antipathy to worldliness; they treasured a devotional acquaintance with Scripture; they sought to develop a spiritual life in private circles of study and by giving their means for the world. They were individualists, separatists, spiritualistic, sectarian among themselves, and many got rich. Doctrine was almost always judged by its effect; that is to say, if a doctrine edified it was true. They had a pattern of "legal terror" and "newfound joy" which was demanded of all conversions; almost as if to say there must be so much of one before there can be any of the other. God was God on the basis of one's subjective experience. Pietism was so inward and subjectivistic that it lost its open declaration of the grace of God for the whole. In character, the real message of pietism became an ethic and not a theology; it was a way of life, not an interpretation of belief. The value of all Christian doctrine was practical. While pietism broke the back of Protestant scholasticism and heralded a return to biblical emphasis, it was not able to accept the new discoveries that resulted from the work of men like Crawford Toy, nor did it have facilities for finding the communion without which church is never church. It could house neither the new man nor the new church.

The fundamental weakness of pietism was its individualism, but it featured also a very unsophisticated view of sin. The pietist theologians were blind and dumb on the master iniquities of human history, says Rauschenbusch. One could hold, he says, the orthodox doctrine on the devil, yet never recognize him when he was seen in a real estate office or at the stock exchange! Pietism did not see the new sins, which included the contamination of milk cans and unjust rents!

Theology has made the catastrophe of the fall so complete that any later addition to the inheritance of sin seems slight and negligible. What can be worse than a state of total depravity and active enmity against God in his will? Consequently theology has had little to say about the contributions which our more recent forefathers have made to the sin and misery of mankind.

Pietists made sin a private transaction between the sinner and God. There was no real consciousness of social sin and evil. Pietism obscured the active sources of sin in more recent generations. Pietism obscured the kingdom of God by its inability to realize the presence of social sins which frustrate the kingdom. Pietism could not see the transmission and perpetuation of specific evils through channels of social tradition. It could not be critical. It did not see the social idealization of evil. It used psychology to interpret the sin and regeneration of individuals but not the sin and regeneration of society. And so "stupid dynasties go on reigning by right of the long time they have reigned." The individualistic gospel, says Rauschenbusch,

has not given us an adequate understanding of the sinfulness of the social order and its share in the sins of all individuals within it. It has not evoked faith in the will and power of God to redeem the permanent institutions of human society from their inherited guilt of oppression and extortion. Both our sense of sin and our faith in salvation have fallen short of reality under its teaching.

Pietism failed to see that our personal transgressions do not develop moral force and resentment enough to slay the prophets of God. It takes public, organized evil to do this.

The pietist was not the new man because his gospel was too small for his world. This man equated the kingdom of God with the sum total of redeemed individuals. Evil was the total of our single sins. He had no notion of social solidarity. His merely individualistic salvation was something less than a true gospel of God. His comprehension of sin was largely limited to acts he did not do, and his propositional revelation provided all that the neofascistic and fundamentalist groups could want. He maintained, mostly, that God speaks what we have already believed that he said. He preserved the status quo at all costs, closed the door to critical social concern, destroyed the possibility of repentance, and attracted the saved and the secure who ran no risks if they could keep their gospel individualistic. The face on the Bible Belt wall was that of a good man, according to his lights, but he was not the new man, and his breed has disappeared elsewhere.

Pietism could never have added up a total of "saved" individuals to produce a "new race of men." The new race does not come that way. Biblically, the genus is prior to the individual—the race precedes the man—the movement is from general to particular—never the reverse. No Jew can think this way; no biblical thought does this. Not even individual churches add up to compose the great church; no individual powers combine to equal the Kingdom; rather, always, everywhere, biblically, the great church is prior to the "church in thy house," the Kingdom is the source from which we came; and the new race of men is prior to the new man. It is given!

I

The New Human Race and the Man Christ Jesus

Bequest from a Premature Century

The biggest accomplishment of the nineteenth century in theology may have been the setting of this frontier pietism on its ear. To the spokesmen of frontier pietism nineteenth-century liberalism was a genuine threat. My boyhood, in the third decade of the twentieth century, was punctuated with attendance upon divine worship; and my attendances upon divine worship were punctuated with jeremiads against Walter Rauschenbusch, Henry Nelson Wieman, Shailer Matthews, the University of Chicago in particular, and other schools in general. It seems that our nineteenth-century liberalism had power to frighten but not to heal.

Yet, in a very real sense, the tools for understanding the biblical base are the gifts of nineteenth-century liberalism. The new human race, implicit in the teachings of Scripture and prior to the new man, is a concept for which we are indebted to nineteenth-century liberalism in a modern setting. That is to say, without nineteenth-century liberalism and its understanding of *social solidarity,* the biblical view of a new human race as prior would have been hard for us ex-pietists to come upon.

Social solidarity was the first of five basic tools used with permanent effect to interpret the tensions that stretch taut between and within the kingdom of evil and the kingdom of God. Their other basic keys were: superpersonal powers, the generation of ideas by social institutions, societal transmission, and social incarnation. Each one contributed to our recovery from particularistic theology.

"Neither alien nor novel" is the claim liberals made for the social conception of the solidarity of the race. They said it was part of the earliest doctrine of Christianity. *Superpersonal forces* have power. (Science supplies the means for killing. Finance furnishes a better method of stealing. Newspapers bear false witness artistically. Civilization adopts covetousness as its moral base—Rauschenbusch.) *Social institutions* generate theories that are adapted to their own welfare. *Social transmission* means that social groups have power and authority to justify, urge, idealize, and redefine wrong and right. *Social groups* can impose moral definitions on their members, and do provide for the operation of powerful ethical forces in all communities. *Social incarnation* is the personification of the spirit of the culture. There are both good and bad incarnations. Thus did Paul's "principalities and powers," able to define evil as good, come back into our view again.

The human race is a great unity from a single head. Sin is not a private transaction between the sinner and God. We rarely sin against God alone. The sins which are really sin need social room to run in. We still crucify Jesus with religious bigotry, graft, political power, corruption of justice, mob spirit and action, militarism, and class contempt. The condition of racial solidarity in sin and the presence of super-personal powers of evil create the necessity for a real Christian ethic. Theological teaching on the origin of sin ought not to obscure the active sources of sin in later generations. Theology must not fail to see the transmission and perpetuation of specific evils through social tradition. Theology must give attention to the social idealizations of evil which create ethical standards. Theology must use psychology not only to interpret the sin of the individual but the sin and regeneration of society and these superpersonal entities. The kingdom of evil means that all men in their natural groups are bound together in a solidarity of time and place bearing the yoke of evil and suffering.

The liberal theologians of the nineteenth century claimed salvation to be the voluntary socializing of the soul. They saw that every new being is a new problem of salvation. But most importantly, nineteenth-century liberals revived the concept of the kingdom of God which held first place with Jesus. I heard Paul Tillich's testimony at Davidson on the effect this notion of the kingdom of God had upon him when he came upon it here in America. "Before this idol," he said most movingly, "I can with fear and trembling say 'yes'!" And it is from our coming to this grand idol, the belief in the kingdom of God, that we can begin to see a new race of men and a new man, the Man Christ Jesus.

Jesus Christ did see that we are involved with the sins of the past, and therefore the guilt of the past. Nineteenth-century liberals did emphasize that Jesus had a twofold belief in the Father, who is *love,* and in the kingdom of God, which is *righteousness.* Nineteenth-century liberals did see that "Faith is an energetic act of the will, affirming our fellowship with God and man, declaring our solidarity with the Kingdom of God, and repudiating selfish isolation." They did see that faith must turn toward its task, and this was to them the social gospel. There was a kind of relativism of salvation, a scale of faith: each is as far from God as he deserves. They rejected the ransom, satisfaction, and vicarious atonement as being alien to the spirit of the gospel. In their views of atonement two ideas were paramount: personality and social solidarity. Jesus cannot bear our sins by imputation—this is unjust. But in the recognition of social solidarity Jesus was bound up backward and forward and sideward with the life of humanity, and in him we see the head of the new race of men.

The death of Jesus has a germinal effect on the kingdom of God. Christ lives fully within the consciousness of God and shares his holy and loving will. He is a new and decisive factor. His is a seminal obedience. His death reveals supreme opposition to sin and supreme obedience to God. *His power gathered by solidarity a new humanity for a new nucleus.* This effects a new thing. In theology it was the clear and insistent necessity for possibility that the historical life of humanity is redeemed.

A long list of subsidiary ideas serves the kingdom ideal among nineteenth-century liberals: belief in the common man, the nature of individual redemption, and the corporate nature of evil; the social responsibility of individuals, corporations, and governments; the concern of God for social justice, the doctrine of work, and the right to work, the evils of parasitism. In Rauschenbusch particularly, the theory of original sin as a theory of transmission means the solidarity of the race, as does his notion of the kingdom of God. The place of social authority in the transmission of sin, the limitation of individualism, faith as a launched journey, and the condemnation of egoistic hedonism implicit in the doctrine of hell, are part of the refusal to take the old salvation for granted and the insistence that all salvation is a single piece of cloth. Once more, the tools are solidarity, superpersonal powers, social generation of ideas, social transmission of ideas and values, and social incarnation. The kingdom of God is the social incarnation of God, though it is more.

In sum, corporate salvation—that is, the kingdom of God —can never be equated with the sum total of redeemed individuals. Nor can corporate evil be simply the sum total of our single sins. It is this devastating notion of social solidarity that gives the kingdom of God its thrust, makes nineteenth-century liberals saints and seers, and condemns mere individualistic salvation as something less than a true gospel of God.

From nineteenth-century liberals we have kept the awareness of the virility of the kingdom of evil with all its shifting forms, its varying modes of expression, its continuing and changeful developments of sin in our own time, and especially its power for redefining good out of intrinsic evil and fashioning new goals. Again, we keep the demands for a responsible society of Christians, which means that the church itself is responsible and involved in struggles that cannot be delegated to political institutions and parties. We keep the corporate nature of salvation, which demands in the name of the kingdom of God an ethic for public life. In the face of the social nature of sin in our racial solidarity, it commands that such an ethic be Christian, no less. The whole is uttered in the awareness of a new humanity from God; the new race of men seen in its head, Jesus, who is the Christ.

Also, the nineteenth century is replete with accomplishments and beginnings. There was the recovery of biblical languages that issued in a forty-year task of exegesis. There was the prologue to biblical theology as we know it today. There was the discovery of the prime meaning of the unconscious. There was the long task of the exploration of other cultures. There was the rediscovery of corporate principalities and powers, the kingdom of evil, the kingdom of God, regionalism, folk mentalities, and national psychoses. The phrase "philosophy of history," first used by Voltaire, became a discipline for use. The field theory of forces in physics, and the new mathematics had their effect on modern theology. There was the discovery of meanings in myth and symbol. There was a great stride taken toward the recovery of the *humanum*. There was the development of social, historical, personality, and value criticism. And in American thought there was the preservation of the notion of the kingdom of God. Along with all these and the clearing work of language analysis in philosophy, we see that biblical theology, historical criticism, personality studies, sociological studies, and ethics would be carried over to a higher level of accomplishment in the twentieth century.

Even so, nineteenth-century theology lost its power to save. With all its talk of Kingdom, it lost its God transcendent. And it lost its God through its loss of its own *humanum*. Nineteenth-century theology did not keep enough of the truly human and understood too little of the only way human beings can talk of God. They did not yet see—indeed, they could not yet see—myth, symbol, legend, and analogy as essential to the vocabulary of humans concerning the Eternal. In stripping the *humanum* of the right to use this tool, in limiting the human to the rational and the scientific, they stripped the God of the Scriptures not only of his feathers but of all bone tissue—no God, no salvation. Precisely here, in the stripping of the *humanum* from God, nineteenth-century theology, both American and European, ran out of power to help.

From General to Particular

No Son without a Father. In overcoming moralistic pietism, the nineteenth-century liberals went too far. The Christ of their teachings had no Father. In simplest terms this was the crisis that called forth crisis theology. How could one speak of the Son who had no Father? There is no relevant Sonship apart from his grounding in the Source. No Father—no Son. Put in other language, how does one go to the nominal, the particular, and the relative, when the universal, the general, and the absolute is lost from polarity?

"True symbolism lies where the particular represents the general," said Goethe. But what do you do with your left-over symbol when the general in which it participates is gone? This was the crisis: the Christ of the nineteenth century was all but Fatherless.

The nineteenth-century workmen tried to fix this and, in their attempts to bridge the gap, lost both wings of the polarity. Some would dissolve immanence in transcendence—swallow history with faith (David Strauss). Others would have dissolved the transcendent in the immanent—they swallowed faith in history (Ludwig Feuerbach). One is the ultimate spiritualization—the other is ultimate humanization. Neither could restore the general (Father), or recognize the particular (Son). Each lost both wings of the polarity. This was the crisis that made Karl Barth stand up. It was not the "war-to-end-war" crisis, or the crisis of German Republican hunger, it was humanity's hunger for the Father.

In his *Life of Christ* (1835), David F. Strauss demonstrates the absurd end to which the historical quest for Jesus could go, would go (faith alone—no history at all). Ludwig Feuerbach, in *The Essence of Christianity* (1841), represents the end implicit in any truly anthropocentric theology (man alone—no God at all). Both Strauss and Feuerbach must be taken seriously. Now that the modern Strauss (Bultmann) seems past his zenith, the modern Feuerbach is upon us—to be taken as seriously, perhaps the only one we have to take seriously; indeed, he may well be the greatest threat with which our generation has to deal. In Harnack, Ritschl, Troeltsch, and other nineteenth-century men, this kind of humanism is laid bare and the contradiction is there, but they were not in position to fix it if they wished. Religion was history, and revelation was σιγή (the great silence). Nineteenth-century theology had lost its general in its particular; its universal in its nominal; its transcendent in its immanent. Feuerbach had proposed simply to reverse the whole process and do away with it all by losing the true content of both terms. Theology fell into pantheism and deism, and this is hard to do. It tears open seams and breaks off buckles and straps. This was the crux that made crisis theology.

Without a truly transcendent God, without a Father, there was no true way to call forth a new human race on the backs of the classic theologians of the nineteenth century. With all they had given, they could still see no new race of men except in a glass darkly. The new race would simply have to evolve— up from the roots of our swampy past—and this demanded no head—just roots in the groundless.

Here in America only the few who read Nietzsche knew that God had died. Crisis theology was superimposed as the third layer on a cake in American thought. There was no crisis deep enough to create such a theology here. We were still quarreling with pietists about a social gospel, which at least spared us the news of God's death until World War I. The cleavage in our corporate consciousness created by World War I, major depression, World War II and its consequent threat to the human race, created such a vacuum that neo-orthodoxy blew into American seminaries and pulpits like a gale. With its emphasis upon revelation, redemption, reconciliation, and with the beginnings of a genuinely Christian and realistic anthropology, its influence on American theological thought is almost beyond estimate. Nor is its work completed. The great validities of crisis theology require an estimate of incalculable worth. It restored a doctrine of God transcendent in history. It met head on and heard the biblical answer as to how the holy God who is very far away could be very near. It heard in terms of genuine incarnation, genuine atonement, genuine reconciliation. But the main work of crisis theology, apart from its use of a vocabulary pleasing to American pietism, was its recovery of God transcendent as a base for its Christocentrism.

Here Barth and Schleiermacher begin to belong in bed together. Here is the crisis for crisis theology. For when Karl Barth became openly, joyously Christocentric he placed the bust of his old antithesis Schleiermacher back in its niche, and well he did, for they belong together and will be read together as "two-century men." Both became Christocentric in midstream. Each turns to Christ to say what he can know of God. Both come devoutly, reverentially; the one with joyous abandon, the other with quiet piety; the one seeing Christ as the only way God has spoken, the other seeing Christ as the most of God he can know. And, actually, both use Christ to keep from speaking of God as "Person." Schleiermacher refuses to do this, and Barth does it with great reluctance and as an accommodation to modern meanings of person not readily available to Schleiermacher.

Without the early Karl Barth we would not need Schleiermacher again. He was buried once (by Barth at that). The Barth who reminded us of the wholly other has in some inverse fashion become like his old enemy when he leads the way in contemporary humanization of the Almighty. From this juncture we can rejoice in his God who is God, face Feuerbach on the wings of the Incarnation; and, if Feuerbach keeps saying that God is man and man is God, we can go a step further to say that God has come as man to deal with our "not-knowing" of death and our "mis-knowing" of evil. On this kind of base, humanism is no longer *mere* humanism. We can now let Schleiermacher speak again. Indeed, underpinned by Barth's God who is God, he is contemporary man whose quiet gracious coming to the Christ occurred in spite of the gap in his time, and who can speak of his aversion to the audacity of calling God a Person without destroying his helpfulness at another level.

Indeed, it is where Schleiermacher is most threatening to the early Barth that we must call him in again. The polarity between the two is a better way to carry forward the issue than is available in Barth alone after he has developed his Christocentrism to the point that the *humanity of God* begins to emerge. From here on out in Barth the contrast with Schleiermacher is not to be so helpful—it is where the great God who is God appears over against Schleiermacher's impersonality of God that the tension makes the need for a clear further step apparent. For the danger now is that a Christocentrism in Barth held so closely to the eye that it becomes a Christomonism will obscure the Father, without whom there is no Son.

For Barth goes too far. He makes God the only person there is. He cancels out his scores of usages of the word "person" by defining it as beyond our ken except in Christ. His Father is the ghostly other where we came in. God is incomprehensible, in spite of fifteen hundred pages of description. Schleiermacher has been reborn in Barth. We go back to the earlier tension to recover the issue, and a sight of the Father. Nor can we use the word "Father" apart from the concept "person."

Why, in their Christocentrism, do Schleiermacher and Barth come together? It is because both use the Son to evade the inadequate concept "person." Schleiermacher excludes the term; Barth voids it, cancels it out of meaning for us, by claiming God is the only person there is. The issue is clearer in Schleiermacher up to the point that Barth seems to me to join him. For Schleiermacher begins at a time when men were just learning that theism could not be taken for granted. Here, where he is most dangerous, where he most opposes the early cry of Barth, he may prove to be most helpful. He may have both a better beginning and a lesser abyss to be crossed.

Schleiermacher, avowed romantic, child of both Pietism and the Enlightenment, carries the seeds of every glory and weakness of nineteenth-century liberalism, but the key is his impersonal philosophy. The fundamental Unity is originally presented in feeling; we possess no strictly objective cognition of Him or It, for the use of the personal pronoun is hardly admissible. God is never apprehended nakedly, but always with or by some finite element of the world. Later, by degrees, he began to use words like the Divine, God, and the Godhead. But neither then nor later did Schleiermacher ever renounce the right to say that *with a personal God outside the world religion as such has nothing to do.*

Rudolf Otto has a splendid defense of this provisional beginning that will not take theism for granted. The world does not suggest simple theism as the only possible interpretation of itself. Schleiermacher puts the question: "There is a divine element in things, have you opened your mind to its reality and answered its appeal?" "A sublime and eternal meaning prevades the world," "has your soul bowed before it in reverence?" Let this be our certainty: "If we first grasp the eternal, in due time we shall discern the Eternal One. If we awaken to the divine, our opened eyes will presently behold God."

From that position Schleiermacher develops slowly "from the divine to God, from an unchanging order and significance in life to the Unchanging One." He goes up this path cautiously. "He will not say one word beyond what he must." (Mackintosh.) He wishes to treat God as not personal at all. The notion of "person" cannot be transferred from the conditioned life of man to the absolute and unconditioned being of the Eternal. For Schleiermacher, to give personality to the Universal Source, this Omnipotent Causality, would be to reduce Him or It to the level of finitude. He cautions us against the error and the crime of calling God Person, as the nineteenth-century men conceived of person. He wishes to treat God as not personal at all. To personalize is to finitize —to do away with God, and here Barth joins him by redefining "person" as a special category for God—the Only Person.

To speak of God as needful—of communion, relation— would be to psychologize on God like any Oriental—unthinkable! It would deny God's goodness. Other Christian theologians are extremely sensitive to how unfitting the word "person" may be in reference to the Eternal.

Hence, Christ takes on absolute dimensions in Schleiermacher, and, I think, in Barth. The aging Barth, in *The Humanity of God,* can only dare this phrase with all its contradictions by making Christ the humanizer of the divine. Christ is the humanity of God. As early as 1926 Barth was interpreting Schleiermacher's Christ as the humanizer of humanity, too. Christ brings us to full humanity. This is now Barth as well as Schleiermacher. Barth has not only pulled alongside the dock, he has moored; he is berthed alongside the colossus of the nineteenth century. Even his total helplessness of man parallels Schleiermacher's total dependency. *Total depravity* and *total dependency* are tandem-hitched, and must be driven together. (Indeed, if one will add the *total determinism* of some modern psychologists, he has a perfect three-horse hitch, a troika.) And thus, coming together, the *classicae theologicae* of two dreary epochs come to a high doctrine of Christ, but this leaves us as needy and hungry as ever for a Father.

Is there no way to a Personal Source (true Father) for the Christ? Is there a way to God as Father who loves, even through the Son, that does not involve God as Person, in some sense person as we are persons? Does he (God) nowhere participate in the highest we can know? Does the Son not demand the concept Father, Person, Love? Is there no way across this abyss?

Not without a twentieth-century extension of a very old theme. We will, given the Son, establish the Person in the Father by a second-century view of the Incarnation.

II

The Face of God?

It is no secret: nature is cruel, man is evil, society produces criminals, culture is marked by agony, and the innocent are victims of pain and suffering. Against this universally known backdrop of cruel nature, evil man, criminal society, agony-pierced culture, and suffering innocence there has grown up in the minds of men an amazing assumption: *that the God who sits over all this cruel, evil, criminal, suffering miscellany of injustice and seeming chaos is a God of Love!*

Where God Is No Person

The assumption about the love of God is a derivative. One does not come directly to it in the history of peoples and religions. It has a long background of struggle. The origins of religion lie in the primitive awareness of mystery responded to by fear, expressed in animism and fetishism. That wide and ancient panoply of nature worship produced by overwhelming awe before the yawning cavern of *mysterium tremendum,* resulting in the rise of polytheism and pantheism, which tried to make enough faces and places to portray and confine the tremendous mystery of God's being, is all subprimary to the amazing assumption that the feared One, the awesome One, the One who has many faces and is everywhere, is One who loves. There is still, at this level, a fantastic span to be bridged before a higher religion can be received. We are in different country from fear and fetishism when we talk about God as Person who loves.

The fundamental structure of all higher religion rests on three primary assumptions: There is a spirit which truly initiates all process. This spirit is characterized by *arche;* it exhibits fundamental order, is true cause of all that follows. All existence proceeds from this spirit, and the true nature of things is spirit. Between this spirit and ourselves there can be relations of knowing and responding. On this tripod higher religion is based; on this structure rests the assumption that whatever power supports the universe is friendly to us men. (Temple.) In this territory begins the famous *quinque via,* the fivefold way of Thomas Aquinas, proofs of the existence of God, elaborations on the framework of that earlier tripod and standard matter for theology, until threatened, if not emptied of meaning, by Kant and Hume. But the way of faith, not proof, persists in the derivative notion that good is more fundamental than evil. That evil is not the primary spirit substance. That evil is a parasite to good and is not fundamental, for God is love!

On this basic assumption rests Judaism and the Judaeo-Christian framework. But the Old Testament never indulges in speculation about the *arche,* as do the Greeks. The Old Testament does not torment itself with proofs or attempts to prove God. In all the Scripture there is no proof for God—the scriptures just *confess:* God is spirit, source, and can relate himself to us. He is friendly to us, so much that we are loved. Good is primary, and God is One. On this base rests Israel's experience, and out of this experience comes the famed and fundamental *Shema* which has for four thousand years called Israel, and us, to worship: "Hear, O Israel: The Lord our God is one Lord: and thou shalt love the Lord thy God with all thine heart." For God is a God of love. That is to say, God is Person.

On the face of it, nothing has been more difficult of belief. It is unbelievable! It is absurd!

Look at the people who believed it, and at their history. They were an unhappy and jealous association of wild desert nomads, caught between the crushing power of the three mightiest empires of the ancient world. They were constantly being overrun by armies, or fighting among themselves. They were victims of captivity, leprosy, treachery, idolatry, and the invasion of other cults and cultures. Their best king was a model of murder, deceit, and chicanery. Their best prophets were stoned, sawed asunder, or made prisoners for life. Their best temple was an unrecognizable pile of rubble throughout most of its history. Their best poetry was about a God who led them into captivity. Their best history occurred before they ever owned a city and wandered wild under Moses in the Negeb. Their best ethic produced a crowd of Pharisees; their best power was the power they had over their women; their best law was an unkeepable demand; and their deepest conviction was that their history was a picture of their own sin rather than a reflection of a malevolent deity. Their deepest philosophy claimed that justice is not the ultimate, and that there is no equivalence between suffering and merit; and although they never accused their God, they crucified their highest and best as if they could at last confess, Our God is absurd!

Or look at the situation in nature. In what millennium did nature change her ways and begin to sing hymns to a God of love? Nature knows no anthems, no hymns, no religious nature songs which see God in birds and bees and sunsets and trees. When did nature change? There have been fifteen hundred floods on the Yellow River in the crowded canyons of China in three thousand years. The Yangtze has destroyed millions in its regular floods. Two hundred fifty thousand died of plague caught from bites of fleas from the backs of sewer rats in Moscow in one season. A hundred thousand died of earthquakes, and as many more of a bomb in Japan. Two hundred fifty thousand died last year of volcanoes, storms, freak winds, and nature's so-called acts of God. In what year did nature turn benevolent and begin to work to preserve us for the love of a God of love?

I watched in sorrow and tears the horror in the eyes of my nine-year-old when she saw a snake swallow a lizard, squealing its terror, and learned that nature is cruel. I look through my glasses from my perch on some high shoulder of the Rockies and shudder at the scream I cannot hear when a wheeling hawk finally dives and sinks its knives into the vitals of a bucking, dodging rabbit. There is this incessant battle between living and the living—between cells and insects and hives and germs. Nature means to kill us, and will likely succeed in the end. Reverence for life? Bah! What reverence can nature have for me—and even Schweitzer must destroy life to save for awhile another form of life. Nature is a world of ant warfare, bee executions, wolf raids, and omnivorous plants. If God is love, it seldom shows in nature. "God! What contradictions!" cries Unamuno, "when we seek to join in wedlock life and reason."

And when we look at the everyday life around us? The situation seems no better. Life seems branded by the conjunction of pain and senselessness. A handsome sixteen-year-old stands in his father's pickup truck and is smashed against a bridge—a friend writes across twenty years to say she cannot answer this—she can only weep with the mother and make coffee for the hordes of friends who come. Down the hall of a pediatrics floor you are almost overcome by the odor of the burned flesh of someone's carelessness. You spend the night on the fifth floor at M. B. Anderson Tumor Research

Clinic and see the miracles of temporary surgery; that old deacon—eight times on the table; the old carpenter, veteran of twenty-seven attempts to stave off cancer's progress with the knife—and you know, even as one who longs to be a man of truth—you know one thing is sure: life is not moved by a law that brings happiness, or by an order that brings justice. You are sure that you believe—but you know it does not yet make sense, and like Tertullian is sometimes said to have done, you pray in a corner in the dark—

> *Credibile est, quia ineptum est*
> It is believed because it is absurd!

Something has been left unsaid. Unless God is Person, in history, experience, and nature, unless he participates with us, is closer than only-Person-there-is, the love we hear about is absurd.

The Face in Event

To this mighty set of contradictions, to this awful frustration, the Christian faith responds with a single Word. God has done something. God has established his Personhood with us in God's Deed—God in Christ reconciling—Christ crucified—risen. "The Word was made flesh and dwelt among us, and we beheld his glory." And this is all we have to go on.

Taken by itself the deed is a ghastly fact; the event, stripped of its meaning, is hideous. "Crucified under Pontius Pilate" means just what it says. But in the light of Resurrection, and their experience of him in Resurrection, in their experience of community and hope and in their sense of calling, they found they had to add a phrase: "Who for us men and for our salvation, . . . was crucified also for us under Pontius Pilate." To their utter amazement they began to see that God had come down and had played the same game according to the same ground rules, even unto death, the death of the Cross. In this strange new light of *kairos* and *kenosis* assumption became conclusion: God had invaded their suffering in his Son (*kairos*) and in response to this matchless Person they became one, united with the God who himself had emptied himself (*kenosis*) to make their suffering make sense.

God had so loved the world (assumption) that he had given his only Son (event) that whoever believed on him should not perish (conclusion!). This conclusion of faith transmuted into its highest expression their experience of God to make their own suffering make sense, since God himself was now involved, participant, at the center. There is still no equivalence between suffering and merit. But this conclusion of Cross event, offered in the face of the basic fact of pain, becomes its one sublime interpretation.

It is a conclusion of faith and of history: this conviction that God himself came and comes into human history in the person of Jesus Christ, "who for us men and for our salvation . . . was crucified also for us under Pontius Pilate; he suffered and was buried: and the third day he rose again."

The ancient world was vastly concerned about understanding, knowledge, beatitude, the experience and knowledge of the loving acceptance of us by God. Paul knew about this; Augustine made it the quest of his younger years. But Paul knew also that you cannot start with law and get the love of God: all you get here is some degree of Pharisaism and an awful amount of guilt. Paul knew the only Christian hope: and so his most meaningful benediction begins:

> *The grace of our Lord Jesus Christ,*

then

> *the love of God,*

then

> *the communion of the Holy Spirit*

Grace, love, communion, this is the order of experience. For apart from the grace of our Lord Christ I cannot find a God of love, nor can I forgive God for nature, and history, and the suffering of the innocent. But by the grace of our Lord Jesus Christ the Christian comes to understand that there is a kind and quality of pain that is redemptive, curative, creative, and this is a kind of pain which man is privileged to share with God. The basic fact of pain is neither explained nor denied—it is just deflated in the triumphant, experienced conclusion of faith—God is love!

And evil? As Dorothy Sayers put it, "Evil becomes the shadow on the world, thrown by the world, standing in its own light whose light God is." Good becomes a resident of strange, dark places, most unlikely candidates are saints, and suffering turns out to be unto life instead of death. God is not mere absolute unchanging. He becomes a participant with me in my own essential incompletion—and provides the good, and the strength, and the will, and the means to make me, in my suffering, like himself—a God of love.

Paul knew this, and so the grace of our Lord Jesus Christ precedes the love of God which precedes the communion of the Holy Spirit and results in some experience of beatitude, some understanding of God.

Our experience is the experience of faith. Nature contradicts us, history makes our faith absurd. Our own experience may be too small or too narrow or too bleak. All the Christian has is Christ.

John Donne knew this ahead of us moderns and closed his own funeral sermon, *Death's Duel,* with the words:

There wee leave you in that *blessed dependancy,* to *hang* upon *him* that *hangs* upon the *Crosse,* there *bathe* in his *teares,* there *suck* at his *woundes,* and *lie downe in peace* in his *grave,* till hee vouchsafe you a *resurrection,* and an *ascension* into that *King-*

dome, which hee *hath purchas'd for you,* with the *inestimable price* of his *incorruptible blood.* Amen.

The Very Human Face

The ancients too, it seems, grew weary with the demand that God be God *in abstracto.* They longed to be dealt with by one who was Father. God as Person is a term of relation, unlike its polarity (absoluteness), which implies no relation. God as Person is source of relation. With them, as with Buber, relation preceded and was distinct from experience. Never in the realm of relation would they "itify" their God— and relation was prior to everything, even abstraction. So they said "Thou"—and to whom or what does one say Thou? In Hebrew there is but one word that means this kind of source of one's being, strength, relation beyond. It is the word for Father. So when they thought of God as relation they thought of him as Source, as Father. But who had seen God at any time? Even Moses? If only God were human, if only God had really been created by father Abraham. Audacity! (Hofmann of Erlangen carried this movement from man to God forward in the nineteenth century until Nygren cut it off, with his eros love so different from agape, in the early twentieth century.) If God were human he would be Father-Mother hovering over us, source of power and love.

God as man? Who could dare think of it? But if God as man were thinkable, if this were carried forward to a term of relation, he would be as Son—and so—as Brother to us sons of God. Son of God—Son of man—same term? At any rate, as Hermann once claimed, God the Son is given! "In Him the fact is once for all established that God does not exist without man!" You say this, Karl Barth, then why do you add in the next line, "It is not as though God stands in need!" Can there not be need between Son and Father—

are all our analogies so empty as this—that there should be need to save God our Father from fatherhood?

It is a twentieth-century extension on a very old theme sung most gloriously in the second century at Lyons by Irenaeus. *He came to us; he became like us*—incredible! He wears a very human face, and our senses can be trusted. "For He did not seem one thing while He was another, as those affirm who describe Him as being man only in appearance."

The Gnostics had intended to settle two problems once for all: the explanation of evil, and the union of finite and infinite. They would do this with a philosophy of appearances and apparencies. Irenaeus aimed to smash this apparition business once for all. He did it with the doctrine of *a very human face.*

> What He was, that He also appeared to be . . .
> not despising or evading any condition of humanity.

Or reverse the words:

> What He did appear, that He also was.
> Unless man had overcome the enemy of man, the
> enemy would not have been legitimately
> vanquished.

Keep him together!

> Those, again, who separate Jesus from Christ,
> alleging that Christ remained impassible, but
> that it was Jesus who suffered.

And as for those who would swallow his manhood—call them *mamuel gulosum:* insatiable gullet—

What he seemed to be, that he was; what he was, he seemed to be! and His work?

> He caused human nature to cleave to and become
> one with God!
> > for unless it had been God who had freely given
> > salvation we could never have possessed it
> > securely.

This is classic incarnation—no equivocation about it. It is set squarely in the context of the living, one, Father God who is Person and who sent him. There is no other, for

such then are the first principles of the Gospel: that there is one God, the maker of this universe; He who was also announced by the prophets, and who by Moses set forth the dispensation of the law— (principles) which proclaim the Father of our Lord Jesus Christ, and ignore any other God and Father except Him . . . but it was incumbent upon the Mediator between God and men, by his relationship to both, to bring both to friendship and concord, and present man to God, while he revealed God to man—

wearing a very human face! This posits a theology of identification. He became like us. And it posits, too, that from which it proceeds; *a Father is established in the Son!*

The goal of this identification, this en-manning is that the very human face of man, brought to the fullness of the stature of the Christ himself, might "be filled with all the fullness of the godhead bodily!"

This humanism, this man with God as man, has even got into Holy Scripture! It is as if God keeps struggling to be born again, as if he must bring something to completion— his own creation—and to do it—wears our face. He became like us—Person.

III

The Historical
—The Human

Incarnation means that the matter cannot be settled apart from history—which includes the history of our dehumanization too. This can occur in two ways, as Teilhard de Chardin knows: by depersonalization and by divinization. We have potential that is actual either way and this is why we are split. Our deepest need is to have this splitness dealt with. Both the splitting and the healing are historical, and human. Paul lists the symptoms of our splitness in the first chapter of Romans:

Godless wickedness; stiflers of truth, with no
defense; refusers of honor, futile thinkers,
with misguided minds, plunged in the dark,
boasting of wisdom, making fools of themselves,
vile in desire, degraded in body, trading God
away, worshiping things, with passions of shame,
through perverted intercourse and depraved reason;
makers of injustice and mischief, with capacity
for malice, envy, murder, rivalry, treachery, mal-
evolence; whisperers, scandal mongers, hateful to
God, insolent, arrogant, inventors of mischief,

without conscience or fidelity, affection or pity,
and *knowingly so!*

This mess is in history and in us. It can only be changed in the same locale.

After a recent sermon one of the ladies of the congregation said that the language of the Romans in my sermon "made us look like worms." At the end of the chapter, after he has dusted off the pagans in a twentieth-century world, Paul says to his readers, Jews and Christians, "What makes you think you are any better off? Your law has made you sinners worse than ever." For paragraph after paragraph there is no mention of Christ in history. Then the healing word breaks on us. Something new floods. The faith that was reckoned unto Abraham will be reckoned to *us* who believe. (Rom. 4:24.) Thirty-two times in eleven short verses the wonderful *"we"* or *"us"* or *"our"* appears. Who are these who are "we"? We are the men of the new creation!

> Therefore being justified by faith, we have peace with God through our Lord Jesus Christ.
> —Rom. 5:1

> When we were yet without strength, in due time Christ died for the ungodly.
> —Rom. 5:6

This is the astounding and ultimate fact at the base of our creation as *we* and *us*. This dying for us is in a class of dying all by itself. There is no atonement in other deaths, there is no atonement in our death, otherwise redemption would be by suicide. That is to say, with Dom Gregory Dix, "The benefits of death do not reach us by means of our own death." Nor do the benefits of the new creation reach us by our own righteousness, and this is the point. Paul's concern with our condition as dying sinners is a perfect willingness to be perfectly honest about a desperate situation. None of us can put up an example. We are all an embarrassment to the human race. (So keenly has this been felt that there was a proposal two hundred years ago in Scotland to abolish original sin by act of parliament.) But here break in Paul's strange words, *"Let us have peace with God."* How? In due time? No more at war with God by tranquilizers? No more at war with God by obedience? No more at war with God by virtue of our own rightness?

The historical-human answer is that here in our locale and time we are no more at war with God because of a Person—in event—in our history.

Can we have faith apart from history? No more than we can breathe apart from history. Is not Christianity the only faith depending entirely on the historical? It is, says Dom Gregory Dix, redemption from *within* history. And this is the point: not by dogma or decree or by fiat of an absentee Judge, but by a very human and historical "wrenching of one Man's flesh and the spilling of his blood upon one particular square yard of ground, outside one particular city gate during three unrepeatable hours, which could have been measured on a clock." And, more, historically and humanly we enter into this being pulled apart; there is no other way or place it can happen; and more, the whole affair is set in such a historical frame that it transcends Bethlehem, Olivet, and applies to his Body which he launched in history like a spear to do his work in the world.

Now—the human truth is this! Where church is Church, something is happening to this splitness, estrangement, this is-ness of ours. In history, as humans, in church, one gets identified with the splitness and with the healing. He is becoming whole. "Wilt thou be made whole?" The becoming whole is in church, and here lies our bitter need.

Here, in history, men may come, rejoice to come, called to come, and identify themselves with a particular man (at a particular gate, square yard of dirt, spate of blood, in a particular time, because it participates as sacrament in all gates, dirt, blood, and time) *to be being made whole*. Here one says, this in me is that in God in history. Here it is possible for me to see my human situation. Here I see the whole man, Christ. Here I can endure seeing what and who I am. The love and courage of the body make it so I can endure this. Here he draws me into his wholeness—and theirs. Here I am becoming whole.

Can this happen in suburbia? I do not know, but it happens in the church. Except that most times I reach for more than I can understand and wind up with almost less than I can understand.

The New Man

Most of today's writers are pretty good at diagnosis, and a frightening list of ailments we've got! We are long on diagnosis and short on therapy. Whatever it is we have had, this malady, we have got it again! Indeed, I think we have always had it and it is a field day for diagnosticians. The cure is a different matter.

Whether one speaks of the fundamentalist banner of the mid-thirties, "Back to God," or Job's, "Oh, that I knew where I might find him," or Unamuno's "God-ache," or the existentialist's "void"; whether one speaks of accepting the inevitable with Bertrand Russell, or of looking for new symbols of new meanings with the theologians, the fact remains—we have got it again. The more awesome fact, we have always had it, abides too. The man who merely analyzes our situation may do some good, but one looks in vain for help as to what to do and where. As for myself, I have less and less hope that denominational houses can offer any real redemption for us. Indeed, most times, as formerly, the institutional church seems somehow in the way. I look for, long for, some radical reconstitution, knowing all the time it will likely be preceded by an inevitable great turning away.

When one tries to talk to this, he is in trouble, he is in trouble if he does or if he does not. There is and can be, I believe, a church that has something to give to this time. There are some biblical categories of meaning that are deathless. But when I tried to speak of this in sermons, I lost my grip. It was not clear even to me! The rocket did not fire; we never got off the pad. I added and added, but the brew would not jell, even though it had cooked all week.

Fundamentally, the hope, the biblical hope, is in new men. But Luther is right: the Word must do this thing and not us poor sinners. The outstanding feature of all our histories is the all-conquering monotony with which man has always pridefully considered himself. But over against all this, there is a relevant biblical hope in terms of the one new human race. The old man, Adam, is reconstituted. He becomes the new man Christ, the new Adam. The biblical hope is the prospect of renewal. A man does not have to die as he is. History keeps taking its hopeful turns on the backs of men who are being made new men. This is a biblical theme and a valid insight. It is the basic category of the new human race.

This is the biblical notion everywhere. All biblical men are Adam or Christ or both. Some of the biblical men are new men when we first hear of them. For some of the prophets the crisis is already behind and is only hinted at, as with Amos, Hosea, Jeremiah. For young Samuel, the being made new came early. For Stephen and Philip the deacon, it has already happened in the backdrop behind our view. Some biblical men reverse themselves, as with Saul and Judas. They are perfect illustrations for William James's "reverse conversion to avarice." Some biblical men halt midstride. They never quite come on through, as with Hezekiah. In some we see a long, continued change in process, as in the making of David the king. That is to say, we see new men being made.

This is the new creation. We see the hammer marks of the mansmith in Moses, David, Thomas, Simon Peter, Paul. And once, at least, we get an epitome of the whole process where we see the old Adam being made the new man in Jacob at Jabbok.

The hope God has, Ephesians says this is where God gets his glory, is that the old Adam can become the new man. The *humanum* must be evaluated, described, projected in the light of the highest we know (Christ), rather than in the light of the *first* we know (Adam); but the first must not thereby be neglected. Adam is the *summation* of a history, not the beginning of it; he is head of nothing. He is just Adam. The garden of Eden is not primal—it is formal—universal— everywhere repeated. We are always in the posture of rejecting our situations of order and boundary. The primal, the point of departure, is really the man Christ—the new race of men wears his face! The exhilarating, confounding, exalting archglow of revelation in Christ is that no man must be Adam. We are not constrained here and, *the problem is not our finiteness—it is our sin.* In Adam we find our history and our past, but not our prototype, says Barth. Adam is our past —but not our "essential and original nature." Adam must be interpreted in the light of Christ. The primacy of Adam is no primacy. The categorical imperative includes Christ's calling of Adam, too.

In Our Hands

The "historical" Jesus and his organic connection with the Church—a projection of his purpose and work in history —the position I have briefed in the foregoing pages—is the position of Dom Gregory Dix. It appears movingly and profoundly in a little book, proofed on his deathbed, entitled *Jew and Greek.* This position stands in opposition to that caricatured in David Strauss and realized in Rudolph Bult-mann.

This position in sum is that redemption and atonement in the world, Christianly, rise from the work, witness, death, and resurrection of the man Jesus who is the Christ who must be taken seriously; i.e., literally and historically, in connection with a particular set of facts in a particular time at a particular place. He is vividly, objectively, actually, factually so!

Bultmann seems to be saying that this one cannot do in this way because the history of these events, times, and places cannot be recovered, if indeed anything was there. The whole is covered up in myth. The relation is not historical but existential and subjective.

The position I will adopt in the next division is that the precise view of neither Dix nor Bultmann contains our best hope. The problem for me is not that of "recovering" the residue of real event out of which theology and a faith can be fabricated. Rather, my problem lies at home and is connected with discovering a base for my own history. That is to say the problem is with history as history. I cannot even recover my own history. *I am a living myth:* images, masks, personages, interpretations, memories, drives, patterns, and values so clutter my consciousness that at bottom I cannot know even me for sure. I am a living myth. How can I expect to do more than bring these myths into orbit around a center? The cloud of my meaning, being, realizing, involves me in the acceptance of the impossibility of history as history. It is an impossible task. The fact of the matter is that I cannot even objectify *me* without wading through a cloud of mythology of my own creation. How can I *objectify* God in Christ in history in such a way that redemption happens?

This demands a subjectifying—the appropriation of the meaning of *Cross-death-resurrection* is by identification of the whole of the Christian event with and as part of my history. The meaning of redemption is no redemption as objective set of standards and facts alone. It demands a subjective relation within my own history. Both his historical and my human are contained in the mythical. The humanism of the thing is that this is all the historical there is anywhere; and the Christ event has objective meaning for my redemption only as I am identified with it.

This is to say: "Whosoever shall carry the Cross, the Cross shall carry *him!*"

Look what happens where the total, factual, *objective* event has been received for generations:

I have the spiritual leadership of some hundreds of "Christian" persons. They are typical of millions of Christian persons, brought together in shared cult acts performed regularly in an historical, actual setting, with membership, participation, symbols, signs, holy seasons, and with dogma, doctrine, beliefs, ethic, and values in common, around their objective acceptance of a salvation done for them, given to them, reserved for them out of their more or less credulous acceptance of the reality of certain historical events in time and place as done by God "for our salvation," and indeed, for the salvation of the whole world, to the maintenance of which setting and values we contribute, under the charismatic duress of a winsome "leader," our regular small checks and our excess bonds if we are building.

We bury, baptize, marry, and meet. What has happened? To fifteen out of seventeen: nothing much that I can see. And to the community? Nothing much that I can see. Here again the problem is worse if we are statistical and objective. So long as we remain in this frame of reference, we have to confess with Christendom that we are like all the rest: no redemption appears. The objective historical factual events of two thousand years ago projected objectively "for us men" into sound institutions do no genuine cauterizing stirring redeeming. We are, in the main, as we were.

Cannibalism, mythological and camouflaged, is now competition, but competition in which somebody gets "et out from behind." *Slavery*, more sophisticated, is now nearly universal, and features many masters for each slave in a world where masters are slaves. *Polygamy* is tandem monogamy. *Monogamy* is adultery where persons are things to each other. Each lives *for* each, *on* each, *after* each, but not *in* each. In all our world of Mecklenburg, and in Charlotte, the "city of churches," not one single, objective, historical church projection of the historical objective work and person of an objective historical Christ has truly taken hold of one single, powerful, effective, objective structure of evil to change anything. The gospel of the status quo is the only gospel we know. And our crime rate per capita and our Bible purchases per capita exceed the per capita rates of Chicago!

But here and there! Here and there! What a different story appears.

It appears because of a real redemption of persons that results from a life of identification.

What if this matter of historical-human redemption is somehow in our hands? This is faith in the active voice and subjunctive mood. How does it happen that our histories, our myth systems, our lives come together? Is this subjectivization not in *our* hands? How does one go from the objectification of these symbols and values in worship to the subjective involvement of life in redemption?

SCENE: The sanctuary

TIME: Christmas Eve in the afternoon

DRAMATIS PERSONAE: The choirs, tympani, strings, brass, woodwind, and organ.

CURRICULUM: Handel's *Messiah*

"And the glory, the glory of the Lord, shall be revealed, and all flesh shall see it together,

for the mouth of the Lord hath spoken it!"

It soars and climbs, beats and pounds, and stops in an ejaculation of silence that is dreadful and I am caught up—my mind and heart and tears and hopes—*filled with his glory*—when?

Reverie

Now when Jesus was born in Bethlehem of Judea there was enough pessimism and despair, threat and meaninglessness, to make all the glorious old prophesies and promises lose their glitter. They sounded like lies. Their cold war was a hundred years old. The old writings were myths, or lies, or dreams, or pious frauds. Only a few could still hope. Only here and there did one ask—"When will the Day Star appear —where is any new day?"

In those pest-ridden days before the Methodists, the queen, and certain politicians remade England, Samuel Johnson noted that "the natural progress of the human mind is not from pleasure but from *hope* to hope." But for that world in Judea hope had diminished—or gone. Yet, then, there was in the womb of a woman that new impetus for two thousand years of Western development and hope—there was then to be delivered from a womb the One who gave the lie to hopelessness. Now again the old hopes sound like lies. Under these myths we cannot even *find* the womb and we look for no new womb to contain our hope. I know now how people lived with the new discovery of a "round" world in the new age of Columbus. It just did not make much difference to most of them. And now? How do you live with a *space event* anyhow? What kind of Christmas could a Marine colonel have waiting to be blown off the face of the globe! How can we make it with a Coming two thousand years away? There ought to be some way a man can live while waiting for the future—any future.

Does not the Christian faith begin in our living with a promised hope, a pregnant womb, an event, a coming that issues in a confident expectation? But when does it come for *me?* Filled with his glory—when? What are the signs of his coming? Where is *my* second blessing? When *my* baptism of the Spirit? Who or what can melt my cold war?

"I want a real advent this year," she said to me in the hospital. She meant, "I want to *get with* this hope business." Some pious fraud had rebuked her weeping, saying, "Have you no faith?" "Faith," she screamed it back, *"I have third generation faith!* But it has not saved me from this despair." "I want an advent," she said.

Advent is event. I know that under my myths and his, under our history, there was a womb that housed the hope, but how do you live with event anyhow? You sit and hear it and look at it, and it goes on by you for Whitsunday and the Feast of Lights. How do you live with event? Unless—

Event is introit. It gets subjective. It gets in—and goes on— for advent is exeunt too—"they go out"—together. One must go with the advent, for who can hold an advent? You make room for it by making a passage *through.*

This is the crisis now confronting the objective church. A dead-end street can hold no advent. Advents proceed down thoroughfares! The humanistic meaning of advent, the subjective aspect of advent is *obedience, receptivity, involvement: identification!* I become not so much victim—I am viator, wayfarer, out to open thoroughfares for the Coming—

"Prepare ye in the desert a highway—"

"Man makes society," says old-fashioned Joseph Wood Krutch, "not society man—he can be saved only by being born again; by recovering that respect for his own nature and his own powers, which so much modern thought, scientific and sociological, has tended to deprive him of."

This is the recovery of humanism implied in the gospel of advent. He does not come to a nothing! We must obey some event in a womb that reminds us that our hope is not merely power, prosperity, comfort, and convenience. I am redeemed even as I am redeeming. It begins in the "craning of the neck," the awareness of need that identifies with a call—I begin to hear and to do!

> (*Tall, huge-framed, gaunt; yet queenly, in a rugged dark beauty, early sixties, bearing like a Mother of all Africa, she held the little brass and wooden plaque and us in her huge hands, leaned on her crutch and said, "I've had over five hundred negro children in my little shack, and they tell me they are different because of it— and as long as I can get to my door* I will answer any knock.")

The same week, in the *New York Times,* an article on Martin Buber closes with his words, *"As long as I can answer . . ."* Filled with his glory—now! It is a prospect of obedience— human obedience.

SCENE: The same
TIME: The same
DRAMATIS PERSONAE: The same
CURRICULUM: The same

> "For unto us a child is born; unto us a Son is given, and the government shall be upon his shoulders; and his name shall be called Wonderful, Counselor, the mighty God, the everlasting Father, the Prince of Peace."

Reverie

I could still hear the hissing sound of the s-s-s on *us—* "Unto us-s-s," it went, as John Finlay Williamson had drilled it into the rehearsing choirs—what if this is so?

What if this eternal theme is now in our hands? What if it is unto us that a child is given? It is no mistake: it is *unto us* that the Son is given. And his name shall *by us* be called Wonderful, Counselor, mighty God, everlasting Father, Prince of Peace. What if God has indeed put himself *in our hands?* This is Christian humanism: in no truly effective way does he have these names until they are given to him by us.

We have this dominion! What difference does it make what God has called him between the two of them unless he does indeed and in fact have the same name to *us?*

This humanism involves a new *agency,* as MacMurray shows in his great Gifford Lectures. The new humanism is neither new nor novel—it is just insight into freedom and responsibility for identification in obedience. We have to name him the same name God has named. God has put him in our hands: a child is born, a Son is given, unto us—and we do not know what to do with him. We really are not accustomed to being so responsible for gifts. This Eternal is to get his name and his character from us.

What good is it to say mighty God, Prince of Peace, everlasting Father, unless he is this to *us?* He is this only by us. At our hands he gets his character and his name. And where can we go to be rid of this? The whole church is still in *postpartem* shock. We want to evade this "unto usness." This gospel must be kept *objective:* we dare not let him become subject. How can we protect ourselves from this holy Child?

Reformed theology will help us! We can so overemphasize the sovereignty of God that we smother the agony of our responsibleness. We can evade our humanhood in his Godhood. We can so define grace and love that God never participates in personhood or need—and is so over us that he cannot get *unto us.* We can use the passive voice and the indicative mood so uniquely in our creeds that there is nothing left for us to do or to be. Eli Yahweh, God has given it—and we can sit and watch it till it dies.

A *federal morality* will bolster our rejection of this dread humanhood. Strange that no one ever points out the similarity between Reformed theology and federal control of life and living. We can so delegate responsibleness to central powers that all our charity, education, work, and responsibleness are functions of government—and never see how selfcontradictory we are when we claim divine sanction for our irresponsibleness. Depersonalize the human: God and government are given givers. Consistency demands it and we hear fewer Mecklenburg declarations of independence. Someone might wind up *responsible!*

Our *confederate culture* will insulate us from this holy Child. We will rear him, baptize him, educate him in the nursery of our own localisms, traditions, definitions, and symbols, so that when he is grown he is a Narcissus of our own values ready to reflect the image of our own liking for the elements of our region and values we have treasured.

And if all this fails, we can fall back into the *objective neurosis* by which mankind has always saved himself from his *humanum*. We can hand over our innards to *any* magician. Like Zsa Zsa Gabor to her surgeon, we can say that we really want little—"just take everything out that could ever be a source of trouble to me." We can hand over our "ill-fated freedom" to any agent, political or religious or professional, who can save us from the responsibility for which, says Dostoevski, the "ill-fated creature" was born. We can become incompetent by illness.

With these tools, in our hands, He becomes an It—a thing, a tool, escape, substitute, scapegoat, magician, Saviour, excuser, alibi, weapon. We keep expecting suffering to be vicarious and atonement to be painless. We deny our humanhood in order to escape his divinity!

Jesus Christ derives his character in today's world from those who name him. What use for God to call him beloved Son, if we name him visionary fool? What use for history to call him its center, if we call him useless? What use for the church to call him Lord these two thousand years, if we call him legend? Can we not make his work of no effect for us? Nor is this to defeat the great God when we name him poorly or wrongly. It is suicide for us—not the murder of God; it is the death of humanity—not divinity. And this is the point: it is unto *us* that a child is born, that a Son is *given;* and his name shall by us be called: our first work is to identify with him in *naming* him. This is Buber's great distinction between relation and experience. The prior given name is a relation of identification in which the primary I-Thou is created for us. The prior is a relation—mere experience *itifies*. Who can call a name by experience? You experience an it, you relate to a Thou. We have objectified: we make him an *It*. He is Thou. Jesus, Thou, mighty God Thou, everlasting Thou! This is *given:* that is, it is in our hands or he was not truly *given.*

We cannot sit on the front porch and wait for Jesus to get named. We name him. This is active voice faith. This world does not wait on God: it waits on us. Paul says the whole creation waits on the sons of God to act like it. And if this sounds like orthodoxy, you are not hearing me. This is not a retread of the ethic of pious obedience; it is heresy, this humanism that we have denied, for it is so risky for God to get his glory from *us.*

SCENE: The sanctuary
TIME: Late
DRAMATIS PERSONAE: All gone—except organ
CURRICULUM: Postlude—*Jesu, Joy of Man's Desiring*

Reverie

Bach is a river into which all things flow. He changed everything he touched. I used to think that the signet Bach-Buxtehude on a score meant that some famous student named Buxtehude had edited the old master into a clearer modern mode. Not so. Bach, as a boy, walked fifty miles to hear the *Abendmusiken* in Buxtehude's great church at Lübeck. Then —when Bach touched the themes of Buxtehude—it was never the same music again. But his most joyous music was this *Jesu, Joy of Man's Desiring.* And what is it, for Bach and for us, that at once makes Jesus so much a *joy* and our *desiring?*

111

Just this: that once he has played the music of our *humanum* it is never the same again. He plays on the theme of our relations: love, parenthood, motherhood, sonship; how he plays that melody. A man must live as if God were his Father. A man must live his short days as son of the Eternal. I have come, he says, in the context of 180 verses of John's Gospel alone, to do the will of my Father and your Father. I am come, he says, to do nothing else. And this is the will of my Father—that not one of you should perish.

Sam Buchlender translated for me the pithy inscription on the tomb of that great modern Jew, Moses Maimonides. It reads:

> From Moses to Moses
> no Moses like this Moses

Why, in all the wide world, has there appeared no second comer? No tomb anywhere bears the inscription,

> From Jesus to Jesus
> no Jesus like this Jesus

Why have we not made him again? Why is there not another one, a second one, one in every generation? Is one enough? Is it because we have not made him once yet? Is it because our desiring cannot shape him? Is it because God sends him for us to name him? And is this the joy—that God has met our desirings, of which there are so many? Lover, I want a perfect mate; pilgrim, I want my Zion; sinner, I need to see a saint—so many desirings.

Twice, in that greatest of second-century Christian writings, in the *Adversus Haereticus* of Irenaeus, these words come: "For He did not seem one thing while He was another: what He was that He also appeared to be." And again: "What He did appear, that He also was!"

Must the expected always be the unexpected? Learned modern rabbis have said to me that they cannot give up the Jewish hope, that the Jewish modern hope is still the Messianic age. And remember that vibrant, passionate dream of Utopia, flashing here and there through the sordid, puerile copying of her capitalistic betters by defensive, brooding and jealous communism; and the poor belabored dream of the American eighteenth century. They are all together: Messianic Age, Utopia, American Dream—and it will come. And when the New Age dawns—will it not be as his Spirit? Whose else? Here we will be together, at our best. And when it is seen whose Spirit marks the age? It is too brittle of us to keep rejecting the unexpected. 'Tis arrogant when your God cannot be incarnated because he cannot need or change or desire. Are not our desires his?

(Last night I sat devastated in a Jewish home with Jewish friends to hear a low, heavy, soft-voiced Jew read Carl Sandburg's terrible indictment of Billy Sunday. The poem, once banned and cursed across the country, came alive in his hands—it writhed and twisted; words spit and cursed and tore at Sunday's terrible graceless, loveless creed. But the point: the Jew was reading to the gaunt, 84-year-old, walking-eternal-spirit-of-man — Sandburg himself! "Slower Harry, read it slower—those are terrible words," he kept saying—all through—

And as Harry read I was stunned by the way the soft name of Jesus kept falling in Bachian cadence from his lips. And Sandburg? And Golden? And all the rest, were caught up in the joy of our real desiring as he read.)

'Tis arrogant when your God cannot change. "You Baptist freethinker!" Sandburg scolded. "I've read every line of your Rauschenbusch. He knew how to talk about Jesus! He was no Baptist—he was a socialist!"

But must not the desire of all nations care for people? And is there not incumbent upon us all the demand to *work* for

113

our desires? Baptist and ex-Lutheran socialist and Jewish humanist, can we not come together here? Our real desires lie here. *He has shown us what to want.*

And the word for *desire* is another word for Father—what everyone wants. *Mishalah,* the text reads later, "the desires of thine heart." "Lord, all my desire is before Thee"—and the "desire of all nations shall come!"

But we do not come into this desire of all nations by sitting on the porch waiting for Jesus. We come into this by doing his work. He and our true desires are within our reach. This is a new surge of a new Messianic age, the age of our acceptance of our own potential shorn of the devilish and false reliance on the evasion of our *humanum* through pious mouthings of faith in a God who as God has already committed unto us as men the tasks that lie within our power.

I have to accept the weight of my own divinity. I can desire; cannot all men? I can bow; cannot all men? I can overcome fear, I can pass by hatred, I can come to that table of the Lord; cannot all men? Not only the lion and the lamb, the adder and the ass, but we too, dear Lord, we too! It is within our reach to drive heartlessness from the earth.

Is there a nomination for someone else to follow? I used to think so—but now I know there are days when all Gandhis and Schweitzers are just irascible old men. On the other hand, how does one shoulder the weight of this *humanum*—divinity?

The Weight of My Divinity

In the *Journal* of George Fox, the great Quaker tells that when he came to Lichfield he was overcome with a conviction that he ought to take off his shoes, give them to some shepherds nearby, and go barefoot into the city. Later, a compulsion which he thought to be from the Almighty forced him to cry up and down the streets, "Woe to the bloody city of Lichfield!" As he cried, before his eyes the gutters of the marketplace turned red, and the pools of the city seemed filled with blood. When the fever that had seized him had passed, he, washed and shod again, asked himself why he should have done this thing. Lichfield was no bloodier than any other city. Perhaps it had been his subconscious recalling of an historical event: in the emperor Diocletian's time, more than a thousand years before, at least a thousand Britons had been slaughtered in the marketplace of that city for the sake of the Christian name. Said Fox, as he turned to another subject: "But I leave this to the Lord, and to His Book, out of which we shall all be judged."

My question: What if the mighty injustices of the past cannot be left to the Lord? What if the injustices of all our past do spill over into the present and we cannot get done with them because they get their atoning in our history? What if the sins of the fathers *are* visited to the third and fourth generation? And, what if this means that every baby who was ever thrown overboard from a slave ship because he was trouble, or every slave cargo drowned because a British frigate was over the horizon, has to be atoned for? What if those Jews who died in the flames of the cathedral at York have to be paid for as well as those in Hungary, Austria, and Germany? What if every one of the thirteen million Germans who died during the Thirty Years' War has to be atoned for? What if every curse, every blow, every death, every undeserved agony, every hurt, has to be, by some colossal justice, made right in our history? What if there is a fantastic "eye-for-eye" justice at the root of things? What if you and I have to sweat and bleed and pay for the sins of the Europe of four hundred years ago? What if this moral agony keeps piling up? What if my sin keeps spilling over so that my daughters and their children and their children's children are cursed to continue to live in the presence of an increasingly mounting pile of moral "stuff" gone sour? What if this four-thousand-year fight between Syriac and Greek, which is not yet done with, has to be atoned for? What if the fantastic human life cost of the Industrial Revolution has still to be paid? And what if even the prejudices that exist in our hearts must somewhere be ironed out?

This would mean, would it not, that no century would ever be finished until the last murderer had been murdered, till the last rapist had been raped, till the last cutthroat had been throat cut. Dante is dealing with this problem in *Paradiso*, Canto VII, when Beatrice says, "How just vengeance justly was avenged hath set thee pondering." She is raising the question, Who will justify the murder of the murderer? Who will justify our history?

Is it true that there is a fantastic justice in history which never reaches a climax in any single generation, and that century upon century we have to keep suffering for, atoning for, hurting for, dying for, the deaths of generations gone? Who will atone for the colossally stacked, morally sour stuff of all the nations and of all our living and all our past?

To this, the Christian faith speaks in terms of atonement and redemption. To this the Christian faith speaks by saying, "It can stop. It has been done. History can belong to the redemptive stream of One who *passed through here.*"

In the San Andrés Mountains of New Mexico, in 1934, they buried Eugene Manlove Rhodes, the classic teller of western tales. On his tombstone, facing the sun as it comes to its end between the White Sands and the gorgeous Organ Mountains, they carved the name of his best-loved novel, *Pasó Por Aquí,* and the date, and his name.

This is the story of the flight of a cowboy fugitive who at length, on the edge of his own collapse, comes to a place called Lost Ranch only to find a family of Mexican tenants dying of diphtheria. Foregoing the advantages he had sought —water, rest, a fresh horse—the fugitive stays to save the lives of four Spanish children and an old man and an old woman. At climax, in despair, he lights a brush fire that will reveal his location to the whole world in order to attract help for the dying family. Sheriff Garrett comes to the signal fire, recognizes his prisoner, sees his washed-out condition, understands how easily he could have once escaped, calls him by a false name, and lets him go his way after the crisis is passed. An old Spaniard, asked why Sheriff Garrett had done this, shrugs and says, "We are *decent* people." Then he tells the story of *pasó por aquí* and Inscription Rock.

Inscription Rock is a great wall in a formation called El Morro, the castle. In the spring great torrents eat at its base and deposit huge piles of gravel and sand in one of the twisting chasms of New Mexico. Through this pass opens the old route to Colorado, Wyoming, Utah, and the great plains of the Northwest.

In the sixteenth century the Spaniards were already using this route. When some conquistador, or later, some lone trapper or prospector, passed Inscription Rock, he would cut his name, the date, and the old phrase, *pasó por aquí.* It furnished a last change of address for many men who never returned. It was a sort of post farthest out. It bore witness to a journey a man had made. It meant that if he were never heard from again *Juan Hernandez, himself, in person,* had "passed through here" in 1587.

Now this is what the gospel is about: *passed through here* —Jesus of Nazareth, A.D. 27; and it is cut in a jail wall in Jerusalem; it is cut on a cross outside a particular gate of a particular city wall in a particular square yard of dirt, and dated! Jesus, who is the Christ, *passed through here*—cut in a grave outside Jerusalem.

What do these words mean for us now, today, across these centuries? This fantastic *pasó por aquí* of One who was despised and rejected?

It means that as the freshets in the spring cut into the

gravel at the foot of El Morro, so his passing cuts into our moral sourness, but it leaves on us a burden. It means that "whoever shall carry the Cross, the Cross shall carry him." It means that when it is cut over your grave that you "passed through here," the only chance for you to have borne your weight against the tottering piles of the moral sourness of our history lies in your having *passed through here as a redeemer*. Redemption involves our being immersed in a stream of influence.

Here in America our nineteenth century is unfinished. The American Civil War really fixed nothing—we are still north of God, and south of God, black from God, and white from God. Here in America the blazing agony of two mighty world wars fixed nothing. Still unfinished! Our wars are unfinished. Our insights are unfinished. The great eighteenth-century dream that made us, still unfinished, our goals unreached, our calling the same, and we are still, in our culture, in our time, in our neighborhood, if you please, contributing to deaths that can be atoned only by some life laid down; and to face this is the demand upon the Christian church in today's world.

American theology was stunned by war and by evil, and we fell very quickly for the great dialectical theology of the second decade of the twentieth century in Europe. Our own reformation against the crass frontier pietism that made our denominations what they are had reached its high-water mark at the University of Chicago at the turn of the twentieth century, but we turned our backs on all the social insights of the old social liberals. We forgot, and now we must remember, that there is still new life to break from men like these men of the social gospel. There are tasks enough and places, handles enough with which to take hold, and strength enough, that those who have passed through here shall make a difference.

Meanwhile, what does it matter that these headstones keep

going up? *Pasó por aqui*—passed through here, John Doe, 1923-59. What does it matter, unless somewhere he took hold? What does it matter that your *pasó por aqui* date is now, right now, unless somewhere we become redeemers caught in the folds, and strands, and strains, and aches, and hurts of those whom we have been sent to redeem? Situations beyond our power to atone remain if the community of faith is not immersed in such a stream of influence that our having passed through here will do something about the moral agonies and stench of our times. The same powers, more genteelly now, continue to distort, and twist, and maim, with business tools, with legal tools, with religious tools, if you please, the lives of people whose sun went down before noon.

Inscription Rock at El Morro was passed one day by a lonely cattleman, on a gentle horse, reading some book. The rider, caught by the shadow and the coolness of El Morro, looked up and saw Inscription Rock—*pasó por aqui*, Juan Hernandez, 1587—and a thousand other names of men who disappeared in the vastness of an unknown continent and never came back. What does it matter, except that in the ruins of the ancient missions of the dry and arid West, you can find, sometimes, the same names again where some fellow took hold *where he was*. And so, Manlove Rhodes said, someday, in a contemporary setting, I'll do a story called *Pasó Por Aqui*—and it became a classic tale of redemption.

But what does it matter—except that in our time of passing through here we may have taken hold of something that has the chance to offer a redemptive break to a world which, without this, must live under the weight of its own increasing piles of our sour moral defection. Passed through here: One who was despised and rejected, and whose cross none can claim, except as that cross carries him.

119

Part III

The Image of God
A Theology of
Identification

I

Menagerie and Myth

Who is this he-she who comes to see the holy man? Who is this who sits there waiting for me to rear back and pass a miracle? Who is this who will not, cannot, tell me who he is, but wants me to hear what he dare not tell me? And who are these who sit there on Sundays packed in rows, wearing their faces so that they will never have to discover their true identity?

Why are his gestures so loaded today? Why does he avert his eye, raise his hand, rub his mouth so hard? Why does she say Yes when she means No; what is that repeated sigh, pause, incipient groan? And why does her hand go to her throat so often?

One thing seems sure. He-she is a living and lived myth. He is not what he says; there is more than he says. She is not what she remembers, or wants, or seems to be.

And who am I, with the gall and arrogance of a semi-professional, to sit there as if qualified to listen? My own past is like hers—it is not there as I remember it. My own future is his future in that it will be for neither of us what we have expected. The bad has slipped out of that idealized past; the good will be less than I thought in that idealized future.

There is a great discrepancy between our recall and what was; between our intentions and our performance, our wishes and our actual situation, between what you see and what I see, between what you hear and what I hear, there is a great discrepancy.

Who are we who sit there listening and waiting for some miracle? Who are these "he's" and "she's," these living universals of potential on their way to happening or not happening?

The Anatomy of Our Godhood

In spite of the fact that we have not always known whether to treat man as God or machine, he is neither. Man is an animal. Man is an animal like any other.

(Wispy gray hair flying, colorful silk bandana, heavy tweed suit on a vibrant bony hulk, knobby handsome head with eagle eyes, Carl Sandburg read his own Wilderness *for me—*

"I was under forty when I wrote it—and the animals were alive in me."

At eighty-four, his voice booms and then caresses, he loves the sound *of words:*

There is a wolf in me . . . .
   There is a fox in me . . . .
      There is a hog in me . . . a fish,
. . . a baboon, . . . an eagle, . . . a mocking-
bird, . . . a zoo . . . a menagerie, inside my ribs.

Man is an animal like many others. The statement was logical for decades after Darwin. On the wings of this thesis much was learned. But now this judgment, so shattering in its effect on some theologians and many believers, has been revised, says Julian Huxley. Man is indeed an animal, but he is an animal *unlike any other*. Even if the taint of his beginning remains.

> There is a wolf in me . . . fangs pointed for
> tearing gashes . . . a red tongue for raw meat
> . . . and the hot lapping of blood—I keep this
> wolf because the wilderness gave it to me and
> the wilderness will not let it go.

Unlike any other animal, man can engage in conceptual thought. He can use real speech. He can make sound signs, verbal signs that refer to objects as well as feelings. My dog has a dozen ways of letting me know that he wants food. My child can say whether she will take pancakes or ice cream. Words are tools which carve concepts out of our relations and our experiences. Through tradition and tools, this *homo zoon–homo faber* has come to his position of dominance. Warm-blooded mammal, mind astretch, dominant by virtue of his skills and his cleverness, the only threat that now confronts him from the lower animals is the rivalry in the kingdom of insects, for

> There is a fox in me . . . a silver-gray fox . . . I
> sniff and guess . . . I pick things out of the
> wind and air . . . I nose in the dark night
> and take sleepers and eat them and hide the
> feathers . . . I circle and loop and double-
> cross.

Man, as animal, is the most variable wild species known. Except for his own parasites he can produce more varieties than any other. And, he has achieved his dominance without splitting his species. He makes no hybrids. He has, testifies Huxley, a built-in interchange, a crossbreeding mobility which guards against his falling off into the trap of producing men incapable of reproducing themselves. The only animal carrying the brain capacity necessary for conceptualization is the only animal to stay out of functional blind alleys. Most mammals that have disappeared as a species died from over-specialization—that oversmartness of nature which makes a special hook, claw, or tooth, then suffers a change in the environment which makes the tool useless. None of this, yet, for us, and even our long fetalization and comparative hairlessness are tokens of the difference, but still,

> There is a hog in me . . . a snout and a belly . . . a
> machinery for eating and grunting . . . a
> machinery for sleeping satisfied in the sun—I
> got this too from the wilderness and the wilder-
> ness will not let it go.

The biologist goes further and says that conceptualizing could have arisen only in an animal like us, unlike any other: a multicellular animal of bilateral symmetry with head system and blood system, vertebrate rather than mollusk, and land vertebrate, not water vertebrate. We had to be mammals among land vertebrates, gregarious, who have most frequently just one young, who came to earth to live after a period of aboreal life. Yet all the time and even from here,

> There is a fish in me . . . I know I came from salt-
> blue water-gates . . . I scurried with shoals of
> herring . . . I blew waterspouts with por-
> poises . . . before land was . . . before the
> water went down . . . before Noah . . . before
> the first chapter of Genesis.

The dominance could have come only to the animal that it came to, and that, further, because man is continuously sexed, not discontinuously. Man is capable of great reproductive variability; he enjoys a wide differential in his fertility but his real advantage is his postmaturity. Through the social arrangements made possible by speech, memory, habit, tradition, man has been able to utilize for the benefit of his kind a time of life which is mere superfluity in all other animals. And here lies his real potential. Most land verte- brates lose most of their powers after their period of sexual reproduction is over. Man's postreproductive period is his true maturity. As *homo politikon—homo interrogatus— homo desideratus,* he can make culture wherein to meet his current real threats, cancer and heart disease; but even here in his peace palaces and emporiums—

> There is a baboon in me . . . clambering-clawed
> . . . dog-faced . . . yawping a galoot's hunger
> . . . hairy under the armpits . . . here are the
> hawk-eyed hankering men . . . here are the blond
> and blue-eyed women . . . here they hide curled
> asleep waiting . . . ready to snarl and kill . . .
> ready to sing and give milk . . . waiting—I keep
> the baboon because the wilderness says so.

And here lies the contradiction that comes from the flexi- bility of his brain. Man is the only organism normally and inevitably subject to psychological conflict. This can be in- duced in other animals. It is native to man. On the way to command over himself man discovers that the captain has a way of disintegrating into a "wrangling committee." This animal, unlike any other animal, can be anxious; he can overload, rupture, blow fuses. He can laugh, worry, project, repress, suppress. He is a victim of both his mind and his manners—his abstract general thought, his unified mental processes, and his social traditions. His psychological powers can split him so that his dreams and his validity, his power struggles and his powers of enchantment, never quite come off.

> There is an eagle in me and a mockingbird . . . and
> the eagle flies among the Rocky Mountains of my
> dreams and fights among the Sierra crags of what
> I want . . . and the mockingbird warbles in the
> early forenoon before the dew is gone, warbles in
> the underbrush of my Chattanoogas of hope, gushes
> over the blue Ozark foothills of my wishes—And
> I got the eagle and the mockingbird from the
> wilderness.

And who can resolve my split situation? Here rises our summary distinction. Man has gods, or a god, or God. He lives in orders of creation from within which he can reach for solution to his splitness. The animal in his lair, among his tribe, flexing his postmature potentiality, diverted by the means of his subsistence (family, society, education, economics) reaches for ultimate unity, to bring his flexible brain-splitness together. And here already he has overleaped the rational, and peers into the vast and subterranean other, the numinous, the *Mysterium Tremendum* he seeks to plumb and cannot. The rational would divert him from his myths, but cannot. Eventually and ultimately he hopes that all his mores and memories, expectations and dreams, morals and standards, cultures and kingdoms of concern will revolve around a center in an integrated whole—and he keeps thinking he can rationalize this to pass. But is he, man, responsible? Man, the *decider?* Is he man who is God?

Everywhere you find this animal, he is religious. That is to say, men are occupied with problems of ultimate unity. Everywhere, man lives in conflict and works to resolve his conflicts in his worth-ship. This is part of his great agony, that he may worth-ship a lesser god than himself, but he worships. He may have many lesser gods during his lifetime, but he worships. Luther put it this way, "Man always has God or an idol."

The only reason we humans are not God is that we cannot make it. Most of us have tried. This is why we experience such difficulty living in the limited orders of creation. To be human means to live your life in and among certain orders of creation. Because you are a member of mankind you are involved with a family. But wishing to be ourselves the center of everything, we push each other around in our lostness and frustrations. Being in a family imposes certain obligations. The only way we could evade this would be to become something less than human, for even the monk or the hermit lives on his memories of what it was like to be in a family. In the family I may be at once child, brother, husband, and father, or child, sister, wife, and mother. This only multiplies my inability to meet the responsibilities imposed on me by creation.

In the modern world there is no place I can go to avoid being involved with a state, some political state, some provincialness. This is our partialness; this is our incompleteness. We cannot belong to the whole world, so we belong to a province. Because we cannot live in the whole, we have to live in a section. Because we cannot be all of the city, we have to be a neighborhood. But each of us wishes to be both whole and center, and this is hard on the communion of neighborhood. It makes poor neighbors.

Because we are human, in a family, in a state, we are involved always in the order of education. Now the state, strangely enough, has the responsibility of educating, but it cannot educate. The power that permits the state to exercise the role of educator, punisher, lawkeeper, and so forth, comes down from within the mores and patterns, the life and religion and morals of the people that comprise the state. So the state, a province, a partial, is sometimes mistaken for the whole, but we have to live with it, and wishing to be the whole ourselves we have our problems. In addition we have to live with our own potential, and something is happening to it all the time that we are alive. No matter who you are, where you are, what you are, something is happening to your potential. We feel the demand to become, to achieve, to know, to fulfill, and this requires the order of education. Something is always happening to our potential, but, wishing to be center, one finds it difficult to be at peace as a mere learner; particularly since so much of our energy is spent in the quest for things, the things themselves, or the exchange of things which posits an economic order.

Because we are human, in a family, involved in a state, involved in education, in an economic order, something is always happening to our solitariness, our aloneness, our communion or lack of communion with others. Now religion is where we begin to speak of our solitariness and our communion. It is where we seek in its higher form what we were created to become. The great Hebrew discovery was that God who is One has put his image in us all. We are the image of God. We mean by this, in the Christian faith, that the one who was created is himself a creator. The one who is the product of planning, may plan. The thought one thinks. The made one makes. The loved one can love. The inevitable moral problem is that he always tries to be a rival to his God. He wants to become another God, and he cannot endure this rivalry. He is caught; he is finite, but he wants to be infinite. He is trapped; but he wants to be free. He is limited; but he wants loose. This is both his glory and his agony and this is what it is to be human. By human kind we mean simply these who inhabit these orders in common as an inheritance and an arena.

Here, as image of God, we run head on into a *terrific contradiction*. The one who is born to be like God, never is. The one who feels he can live forever, dies. The one who is born to have dominion over the inhabited earth loses a gland the size of a peppercorn and turns to an idiot. The one who is born to think, and feel, and be, has a stroke and turns to a mass of vegetable matter to be cared for until he turns to mineral. Man is a contradiction: made to rule, he is a slave; made to think, he lives on comic books. He is a contradiction; there is a gulf between me and what I am meant to be. My potential is beyond me. Made to be man, I am more like antiman. Made to be good, I am bad; made to eat, three fourths of us starve; made to laugh, Isaac, the laugher, soaks the earth with his tears. To be human is to be sinner, and we are caught in contradiction.

O, I got a zoo, I got a menagerie, inside my ribs, under
  my bony head, under my red-valve heart—and I
  got something else: it is a man-child heart, a
  woman-child heart: it is a father and mother and
  lover: it came from God-Knows-Where: it is going
  to God-Knows-Where—For I am the keeper of
  the zoo: I say yes and no: I sing and kill and work:
  I am a pal of the world: I came from the wilderness.

(Sonorous and severe—then sibilant and breathy, holding on to the words he liked the best—vowels and consonant sounds in tandem—the old man came to the end and left me with—)

The Myth of Our Humanity

Look at my myths: they will appear in any list of what I want.

The heaven of my fancy would contain, I fear, no pietists, no scientists, no mathematicians, nor any other kind of fundamentalist. It would consist, in the main, of a small coterie of agreeable theologians, not too smart for me, who generally are in agreement with me, and who speak English. There would be few, if any, Yankees, for I find them very provincial; no Democrats or Republicans, for they all sound alike; but a few good stout atheists for spite and for everyone's amusement.

As for women, there would be a few: my own wife and daughters, not from duty, but because I happen to like them; the wives of some of my friends, but not all; a few enjoyable female seekers and theologians whom I have found to be able to disagree like gentlemen, and then, a few for decoration. My mother, of course, if she really liked it and decided to stay, and a few of the children whose love has made the pastorate worth the trouble.

My heaven would include my father, because he has never in all his life presumed on the Almighty just because of his faith. It would include almost no theological students, for they are arrogant and know far too much for my heaven. There would be a few rascals, one *carajou* mechanic I know to fix things where he couldn't charge for it, a deacon or two, most of the men I have worked with, a hunting buddy, a few animals I have loved, some trees and a river, mountains and a moon, and frost and fall and summer. There would be some odors, some memories, and a few unanswered questions to push around; no games, no puzzles, no charts, no calendars, no engagement pads. I would include a few books and one or two writers I have read a lot; a Catholic priest I knew in Korea, an old uncle who would be so surprised he would be fun to watch; no germs, no debts, no money, no Brussels sprouts, no elections, no High-Church Anglicans, no professional pastors, no denominational experts, no finance campaigns, and no Saturday evenings without a sermon ready.

No linguists, no faddists, no experts on anything, but I would need a good flutist, a good organist, and one real tenor. I'm not sure yet about real Presbyterians, or Disciples, though many are an agreeable lot, and one or two salesmen because of all they have to put up with and for Willie Loman's sake.

I would take a boyhood friend or two, a good saddle, a good knife and a hearty appetite, but no pills, tranquilizers, hair curlers, tweezers, or stiff petticoats.

How absurd, you say. How profane, how limited you are, how provincial, how insular, how little can you get? Heaven is not safe in your hands! Precisely, and neither is life! In spite of all man's vaunted adequacies, neither your life nor mine is safe in my hands. I am not competent to decide the constituency of the eternal, nor are you. There are too many myths.

In this connection, of man and myself several things seem clear: my past is not there as I remember it; most of the bad has slipped under somewhere. My future is not as I expect it; much of the good will slip out somewhere. What I recall and what was are not the same; what I have intended and what I have done are not the same; where I have gone and where I have wished to go are different. What I see me to be and what I am seen to be are never the same. What I hear me saying is not what you hear me saying. Where I see and where I am seen are in separate contexts. What I feel and say I feel are not the same—and what I say is not necessarily what I think, and vice versa.

My hope is as much to conceal as to reveal; the wish to hide and be hidden and to keep is the same. My courage is my fear in a corner; my virtue is my fear on guard; my laughter can be derision, or a curse, as well as communion. My prayer is a cry, preaching is confession or arrogance, and my pride is myself as I wish I were.

My involuntary actions mean more than my words. There is a truer meaning in my unintentional use of loaded words than in my careful composition. My tone and pitch say more than my syllables. My skin and my eyes, my pulse and my viscera speak with a truer tongue than my brain. My rational is only true when it is painful to me, and but partly so then. My conscious is deceived, my conscience is a biased censor, and my floriate cabbage leaves of subterfuge cover my core. What I think I am agrees with no one else, and I will not, dare not, cannot isolate my own who. No one ever reveals all his inmost thoughts. My fantasy thinking is as meaningful as my rational thinking. And what is worse, since I have read a book or two about this, I am always taking off the lid to see what's cooking.

In all his relations with his kind, man swiftly breaks through the crust of the rational to the molten emotional lava beneath. The greatest human phenomenon of the last fifty years may be, not the growth of religious unbelief, as some have said, but the decline of the rational as the real core of the *humanum*. Whatever *ratio* may be, it is as shell, not as center, it is as mask rather than core, that it appears. Whatever the true center of the self may be (if indeed the self is not a field-in-relation rather than an integer), it is something other than our rational powers. For reason, "the great whore," will serve any of our desires and emotions. There is a deeper center.

In this twentieth century, as Mann pithily shows, the reaction against classic rationalism and intellectualism has been sparked by a kind of hatred for mind itself. "Man has greedily flung himself on the side of 'life'—that is, on the side of the stronger—for there is no disputing of the fact that life has nothing to fear from mind, that not life but knowledge, or rather mind, is the weaker part and one more needing protection on this earth." This situation indubitably must change. A recovery of the rational is as serious a need as the return to emphasis on the conscious which has but recently been felt in some European psychological circles. But for now, in this present human situation, the rational has a hard time of it, and even Reinhold Niebuhr sees the caldron of the pretensions of the heart as the source of our darkness about the self rather than the finiteness of our minds.

Without some sort of triumph of the rational, man cannot

survive his own emotions, but neither his mind nor any other term for rational power has determined his present stance. Augustine, in *De Trinitate,* saw the priority of something extrarational, and longed "to see with my understanding that which I have believed." It is as if mind has already been preceded by manners or acts, insofar as control of deed by the rational is concerned. In Don Quixote's battle with the lions, the old lion's lazy disdain, not Don Quixote's bravery, saves him from dismemberment. The man in the green circus cloak covers this and most of our human situations: "What he said was coherent, elegant, and well said; what he did was extravagant, rash, and foolish." And is this not ever the way with us? "Viewed from the heights of reason," says Goethe, "all life looks like some malignant disease." Yet it isn't.

For life is not mad; it's a *myth.* Even Karl Barth's "man of flesh and blood" is a myth. Real living is the "reconstitution of a myth" through which life becomes genuine and authentic. By means of the building of my myth I remain in touch with my center, or rather I am able to abide within the field of myself and my relations. Significant life celebrates a growing *mythos*—this is the meaning of the "Who am I?"

That is to say, life is a lived myth. It is a shaping which features the merging of myth and psyche in a field of relation which issues in a person. Thomas Mann's word for this is *Bildung.* Seen from inside, it grows up layer on layer. Its subjectiveness is its participation with its whole being, as Tillich says of theological subjectivity. It begins in earliest infantilism's success or failure to identify with a myth that will shape as it goes—nursing and weaning, receiving and grasping, hearing and responding. This is what some were saying years ago in despair with the liberal doctrine of man —in depth psychology we will find an undeveloped anthropology. And it is the anthropology of a subjectivistic morphology of myth and psyche. Each lives in a cloud of changing myth.

What myths we mythe—or as MacNeile Dixon puts it—what bubbles we blow! The hero, the lover, the frontiersman, the saviour, the healer, the mother, the nurse, the pilgrim, the hermit, the preacher, the lawyer, the entrepreneur, the rich man, the thief, the virgin, the wanton, the saint, the father, the strong, the dependent, and the pure. What myths we mythe?

To be person is to be able to share your myth—to share many sets of myths—to move freely in and out of living myths. To see life as religious, as feast, as celebration, as a dance of life and death, as myth, is to see it as it is. To be person is to be able to move through the limitations of your own mythology to a larger one. To be person is to be able to be open to the reading of your own discarded myths which leave their rings of skin and cartilage behind. To be person is to be living the life Ortega y Gasset calls "open-ended behind" life. It's to have entrance and exit. To be human is to be living with other sets of living myth in acceptance of the complexity of the overlap. To be person is to be field of relation in relation with other fields of relation by way of myths held in common.

And not to be person? Conversely, it is to be fooled by your own myth. It is to have mistaken the mask for the man. It is to hear the words instead of what is meant. It is to be shallow, unaware of the silent signs, the signals, the lights being sent out by other powers in the dark. Not to be person is to be alone in your own myth system without knowing it is myth. To be un-person is to be unhearing and unheard through your preoccupation with your own noises. And sometimes the preoccupation is a frustration with a myth of yourself you cannot get straight; it keeps slipping askew over your aggressions and hates and denials.

Why does a woman at forty clasp her right hand to her chest when she says, "Now, if you ask *me*"—or "All *I* can say is—"? What is the long sigh, the drooped lid, the fast-moving left hand over the hair, the clasped lips, the pause, the averted eye, the agitated lid, the stutter, the slip in speech, the angry denial, the too eager affirmation, the slower stammer?

Who is this he-she who sits there waiting for me to be magician and carry away the troubles he-she has not told me about? Who is this who I must hear until he-she is Thou. Who is this whose blandness I must somehow hear past me until a living person can come to be? He-she is a living and lived myth. But the myth has some corners, intersections, encounters, places of meeting, lines of tension, scars, threats, fears, loves, breaks, hopes—or how would you say it? It has and is a myth with seams, lines, tears, segments, sections; threads and cords run through this field-in-or-out-of-relation.

There was a father and a mother and a lover—problems enough—or—there was not a father and a mother and a lover —problems more. Or there was one and not the other, or there was the other but not the two that remained lacking. There was a father who was or was not father; there was a mother who was or was not mother; there was father and mother, one or both of whom may have been or may not have been. Not to have been may be as great a boon as to have been. There was a lover, or lovers, or no lover at all; a lover, or lovers, who should not have been, or who were and then were not. There was a brother or a sister, or brothers and a sister, or brother and sisters, or none at all. There was or was not a friend or friends.

There was eating and waiting to eat; there was hollering and swallering, falling and being held, sleeping and waking and wanting not to sleep or not to wake; there was a time when it was all right to wet the pants and then there was suddenly a time when it was not all right to wet the pants, or perhaps there were not pants and never a time when one could not do as nature asked. There was nursing and weaning, or all nursing and no weaning, or too much weaning and too little nursing. There was love and acceptance along with authority and rejection, or there was not. There was peering curiosity, rejection, acceptance, mystery, threat, fear, rivalry, repression, hurting, shame, delight, torment, comfort, misery, and there was SEX.

There was incest and murder, in embryo, for this is what it is to want your mother and reject your father—or be wanted and rejected. There was anger, there was frustration and denial, there was license—and above most else, there was dark, there was pain, there was surprise and shock. There were gangs, groups, bullies, buddies, teachers, little girls with strange odors, ugly words you thought and heard and learned to read on walls; there were dogs and natural acts which were made ugly by sniggers. There were pictures and books and timid graspings and experimenting, habits and secrets and jokes and glimpses. Dreams, maraudings, rapings, nightmares of fantasy—and—there was *GUILT*.

God and good, Sunday, starch, teachers again, stories, words, boredom, mystery, fear, old men and women, and symbols. Rebukes, decisions, repressions, regressions, recessions, projections, approaches, reproaches, encouragement, assault, boredom, waiting, dreaming, hoping, finding and not finding and not being found.

There was beauty, wrong, pride, despair, hilarity, hysteria, decision, danger, and jealousy. There was memory, expectancy, hope, and forgetfulness. There was security but then insecurity. There was permanency made temporary, and things that would not stop. There was pulling, rebuking, smacking, threatening, and demanding. There was ignorance, fright, prejudice, a hurting conscience, and there was No, always there was No. And there suddenly, one day under the tree, neck broken and limp, or by the roadside, or under

the porch in the dust, there was DEATH. Who is this he-
she who sits there hoping for a miracle?

He-she is a living and lived myth—who cannot tell me all
this, and this is not all. He-she is a whole world of potential
on its way to happening or not happening. He-she is an incarnation of all the divine and human there is, he is more or
less, sick or well, split or whole, depressed or jubilant, sinner
and saint, Adam or Christ or both, and somewhere in between. And *the only agony he can know is the agony of a
threat to relation.* The only place he can hurt is in some tear
or split of relation within his personhood. He cannot tell me
this as yet—but if I can hear it there is healing to be had,
perhaps. But meantime there he-she sits in his myth—and
if he-she is myth, what am I, and God and Christ and life?
The hurting is in some seam of the myth where relation is
pinched or threatened or torn, or pulled out. There is no
other human threat except that of estrangedness, splitness, to
be cut loose from potential in relation. This is sin and death.

And so, in and through and past the torrent of words, one
listens for gestures, loaded words, signs, whimpers, sighs, signals. Someone is waiting to be born.

Trim and charming, western openness, eastern fashion-
able finishing, smooth and good to look at; artist, sensitive,
cool, unbending, all the right words in place, but no "curriculum" on the table yet—reluctant, withholding, a little
embarrassed—

The myths flow by you: great drawling open western per-
missive father; small, petite, but hard and ambitious social-
izer mother; much-loved and well-favored brother; happy,
happy girlhood; virginal innocence, proper rearing, sterling
character; artistic talent; career from college; pleasant proper
husband—darling dimpled daughter.

The topic on the table: *Christian baptism!* Why certainly
so—what a gracious, beautiful, and fitting subject for this!

139

THE RECOVERY OF THE PERSON

Time to get with this Christian business for the child's sake.

But you haven't heard her yet. The hand to the breast and throat too often, words of affection a little *too* loaded; signs you cannot verbalize, the air of recitation—the formulas of propriety—

Listen, listen, wait:

Why does her hand go to her lower throat when she says *"All* I want," or "with *nothing* to fear," or "with all my heart"? Listen for the thread. It will appear in the context of a relation.

And there it is—the ravel of yarn that means a broken seam: "This darling little girl . . . the least I can do. . . ." (Hand to throat, eyes aside.)

> *"She means so much to you?"*

And it begins, haltingly, painfully, then—

> *"Why do you put your hand there, Are you keeping something you want to tell?"*

And when it's all on the table, after hours, look at our myths again!

Back of the little daughter . . . frustration of desire for sterility . . . to ease a terrible guilt . . . extramarital . . . hatred . . . husband neglect . . . loss of virginity . . . revenge against all men in one man . . . Daddy did not help me . . . five-year girlhood torment . . . fear of pregnancy . . . fear of blood . . . trapped by an old hired man

high there in the wide upper hall of that huge broad house of the mythical setting of her constructed perfect relations with her kin—there where she had buried it—it lay on the tip of her tongue—

her mother's own brother!

Now what surface baptism can wash away *this* bit of information? This scar, this fissure, this hole in the wall of personhood demands a mighty healing—a crucible of redemption at work in the world.

The name is Legion, for we are many. And this is the existential situation in which and from which our myths so protect us that we cannot recover our own history. Even in the nice ones the id is pure dynamic, irrational, knowing no good or bad or time or value, only desire. Here, where we fight like rodents tearing gonads, our primitive demands survive decade upon decade—to get to them is like defusing a time bomb (not work for an ignorant though pious clergy). And around this id is the ego; trusted to procure my desires and look good in the process. Unprotected from the world of the id—naked to mine enemies—except for the delay of thinking, experience rationalized, correcting—ego swings in its lonely orbit, and only thou and Thou can intervene.

What limping and namby-pamby reflection of unredeemed values and mores, meeting regularly and muttering its hymns, lisping its myths and obfuscating its real situation, but calling itself church, can hope or even want to deal with this kind of human being? Yet this is man as he is in his myths.

What denominational project and educational program with cultic implications and cultural appurtenances can bring this split man together? What mere institutional loyalty and pious affirmation of myths can afford the meeting of this I and a Thou who can heal him? What church can endure the torturous heating of fiber necessary for any annealing of this splitness? No ordinary one, I'll grant. For this hope, a crucible of redemption is required.

II

The Crucible of Identification

They were wrong who said I was in His image because I could think, or love, or hope, or seek, or laugh. Nor am I in his image because I can and do suffer. All things that can remember turn home at eventide, and all living things that can turn homeward can suffer. But only man can ask why he suffers, and thus find himself in the crucible of redemption. It was a man being redeemed who wrote from home, after eventide, while most else slept,

Why is suffering so fruitful—and joy so barren?
Why can I so quickly forget the moment I laughed
and remember so well my despair—and tears?

I hate tragedy's fruitful womb—
I shrink from sorrow's turgid breasts
When God's child comes closest to livingness
Why is he closest to death?

Can spirit-ternal love only be born
on the abyss of extinction?
Has anguish more common-ness than ecstasy?
Damn!

This was not meant to be
Whose rough hand has done this?
There *is* sin and redemption and the eternal conflict
This ghastly struggle—Cross versus empty tomb

But cannot life marry joy and beget children?
Does only the prisoner know freedom?
Could not, cannot the free man know freedom
unscarred with chains?
Does a man hear his Ninth Symphony only
when he is deaf?
Why cannot the bearing man bear higher (if
life is a blessing)?

If life is reality and no phantasy
Why does it so well in the shadows of dissolution?

Is this God's private domain—Has He shut this
  door to me?
Can man not enter here?
Would bricks made from this land's sand
Build a tower that would reach?
Does creation beget a child so
imperfect that he must die
before he can begin to live?

Now, Sir, I am past two score and
I no longer fight the mere situational reality.
Rather I inquire about intention—primal purpose
Did this have to be *potential?*
Else why would my well-fed child stir in sleep
As my sick child stirs in his illness?

Man has *two* hands and he looks backward
only when he turns his head—
His eyes are on horizon level and he knows words—
Nothingness, becoming, too. But there is also a word
called "being," less digits, as much breadth
and could a man stand here?

Stand on what, John? The fact of suffering or the refusal of suffering; the threat of death, or the refusal of death and the transformation of suffering: Being, or the splitness of being, or the refusal of the splitness of being?

> Do not go gentle into that good night,
> Old age should burn and rave at close of day;
> Rage, rage against the dying of the light.

I heard the near-dying Dylan Thomas sing it—and Unamuno and Berdyaev.

Is this not our *Imago?* That we will not accept suffering and death? That we so regret it and resent it, and have so ached for the power to change it that we have hoisted our very God on the petard of this hurting splitting of the id in order to anneal our divided and warring selfhood-Godhood?

The Divine-Human Crisis

The memory and the expectation are as one. They have to do with what it is to be at one. And out of the abyss that cleaves us, between *ouk on* and *me on,* notbeing and nonbeing, the not-at-all and the not-yet, there rises a symbol of the very splitness of *God who is like us.* There, hoisted on the center prong of our splitness, spread-eagled, where the Eternal is pulled apart, not to keep us from being pulled apart, but because we are pulled apart, he keeps hanging to make our suffering make sense.

This is pure subjectivity, this is total participation, this is Real Presence, this is identification—he became like us! To show us who we are! That God is like this too! That it belongs to freedom, and the power to decide—and that we have to *decide:* whether we suffer unto life; or suffer unto death. But suffer and protest we shall—till things are right! This

is what it is to be a self, agent, free, responsible, moral, aware
—aware of the contradiction in things. He is like us—we
are *imago Dei.*

The Cross for us Christians is the hyphen of the primary
word I-Thou. This is where we come to receive our I-ness by
receiving his Thou-ness, and to lose our It-ness by losing his
objectivity in a common subjectivity. Here we are called to
accept and participate in the wholeness of things. Here our
history, which we cannot recover, is caught up in his, which
we cannot forget or recover either. Here emerges the truth
of that taunting one-line epic on the restroom wall in a new
building at the University:

God has cancer,

it says.

And the answer? He has had this a long time. Why has it
not killed him off? He has become like us. Here our myth
systems meet and we *identify. Eli, Eli, lama sabacthani,* he
cries from the cross, and it is a cry of identification: with the
22nd psalm, and Messiah, and the Father's will, and with us
—for here he takes his ultimate stand with our suffering and
death. *Lord, when thou comest to thy kingdom, remember
me!* And this is a cry of identification too. The arrogance of
our projection is exceeded only by the grace of His acceptance.

"It is less terrible to fall to the ground where the mountains
tremble at the voice of God, than *to sit at table with him*
as an equal; and yet it is God's concern precisely to have it
so." And this is identification—but how can it come about?
How does he become like us—subject—present with us—
identified with the *imago Dei* that suffers?

The demythologizing of the gospel of God is a terrible and
lonely business. It is a part of another demythologizing—the
stripping of myth from me, and this is terrible business, too.
This stripping of gospel and self is a prime necessity only for

those who cannot endure life as it is and who keep seeking the clarity of the rational; who keep having to see what is under the altar cloth and the bed sheet. For these curious ones, these rational ones, shorn of language, symbol, myth, analogy, and all attempts at concreteness, stripped down to primal language, does the gospel not still speak of an Other who has so come to meet us that this Other participates in us, surrounds us, invades us, and calls for a communication—a responding—a word? Is not the simplest remnant left from our stripping a word of Being-Love who comes to meet us?

And as for me, tear away all the images, bulwarks, emotions, masks, roles, and cabbage leaves we hide behind, and is there not this remnant? The core of a yes and no, a will, a decider, who either must look toward the Other or turn his head? Stripped, is there not left to us choice of some kind? Is this not the essence of our freedom—our divinity—our manhood? And is there not portended here a meeting, an identification—where will chooses and submits to having been chosen?

Søren Kierkegaard made this choice the very passionate heart of faith. I wish to make this capacity to choose the very living heart of the myth that is me—and call it will. The welcomed invasion of my will by Other constitutes my identification—but when I explain it, all my myths and His come back into the picture, for naked will and abstract Love cannot find an expressible bond—so I enflesh them again to see them and lo: Cross and suffering and me and suffering and God and Cross and me are still in the same frame. The arrogance of our projection is exceeded only by the aptness of the symbol event that has caught us. But not to me or to mine alone. This identification of Cross and God and man is for "whosoever will whom the Lord doth name." There is, as in my suffering unto death, a fellowship of suffering unto life.

The Cross, for Christians, is no *ransom* paid to a Satan

who would have to be as strong as God to be bought off this way. The Cross is no *penalty* paid to satisfy the justice of a God who would outrage justice in the very acceptance of the suffering of this innocence. The Cross is no *vicarious* suffering and dying, not a *substitution;* for who has been saved from suffering *and* death? I cannot find that Satan is so strong as this, nor that God's justice could be as perverted as this; nor can I find any relief from the suffering and death this gaunt but hopeful specter, freedom, has imposed. Rather, he has become like us, his cross rises up out of the same bed upon which we already suffer. He suffers, not to keep me from suffering, but because I already suffer and to make my suffering make sense. The Cross rises out of the abyss that has split me; it splits him; he has identified with me—and here at the sign of his splitness, I identify with him. He is me—God has come. And he dies by faith, not knowing, but believing that the Father would raise him. He dies like I die, lest he pull his rank on me, believing that the Father would call him from the grave. He became like us—no abrogation of Incarnation at the end—all the way, like we die. Who would not die for the healing of the whole world if he *knew* he would rise in just three days?

The Cross—universal symbol—because true in every village, because true in every man—this is where we meet. This is the essence of identification. It's not the old cry of Barabbas, "Jehovah! That's my cross he's dying on!"

Rather, this is the cry:

"Jehovah! That's *me* dying there!"

He became like us!

So he hangs there because I already hang. He suffers because I already hurt. He endures there because I cannot endure alone. He cries as I cry. He dies because I already have to die. *Eli! Eli!* There, hoisted on the center prong of our splitness, spread-eagled, where the very Eternal is pulled apart, not to keep us from being pulled apart, but because we are pulled apart, he keeps hanging to make our suffering make sense.

Pure subjectivity? Is it now? This is total participation. This is total identification. He became like us. Irenaeus repeats himself,

> What He was that He seemed to be
> What He appeared to be—that He was!

He became like us, to show us who we are; that God is like this, too. That it belongs to freedom and the power to decide: to suffer life and death, to be self-agent-free-responsible-aware—*imago Dei!*

The Cross for Christians is the hyphen of the primary word I-Thou. Here we receive our I-ness in his Thou-ness and lose our it-ness in a common subjectivity. Here our history, which we cannot recover, is caught up in his which we cannot forget. Here the arrogance of our projection is exceeded only by the grace of his identifying. He became like us, and there you are! *Ecce Homo!*

> split, stopped, halted, crossed, cruxed,
> estopped, drained, split, laid open.

There you are. And it means nothing for our salvation healing except as we identify. He became me—I become Christ. Not *imitatio Christi,* says Paul Lehmann, but *sequentia Christi,* and this is so.

The Community of Relation

Out of this identification of divine and human in the crisis of suffering which is Cross there issues a continuing divine-human relation—a fellowship of suffering unto life. This is the church in the *nominative case.* It is the name of something we can see, taste, feel, know and belong to. The church has a *genitive* case and this is relation. It has a *dative,* and here it is instrumental agency and has *means at its disposal.* It has an *ablative* case and this is its realm of *witness,* for from the church something flows. And, the church is *accusative* too, and this is what it is to God, objectively, for this nominative, genitive, dative, ablative, this agency, this relation, this instrument, this witness, is in the accusative as a direct object to God, the realm of the Holy Spirit's work. This relation, rising out of the divine graciousness—over and against human arrogance—draws its breath in the living presence of the Holy Spirit of God.

The community which is the arena, the relation which continues, the means at its disposal, the witness-work of its calling reaches its objective in the Holy Spirit of God which *is* the Spirit that makes *and* resides in holy man. This communion of identification, the church, is child of, and tool to, and abode of the Spirit of God in his life in man. The life of the church is a genitive—a relation—the term of our relation is the Holy Spirit. In terms of Christian humanism, to say the Holy Spirit is to speak of the informing, constituting, relating, using, witnessing Spirit whose presence makes this community like nothing else on earth. It is in the context of his presence that a poor and otherwise ineligible illegitimate may occasionally come to himself in pulpit or pew and say, not irreverently, God Almighty, I'm in *church!*"

The Holy Spirit is concerned in the church with the kind of oneness that *is* holiness. This is what it is to be well: to be holy, to have all parts present, centered, functioning in the right order. This order of holiness is being arrived at in redemption which begins in moral *awareness* (i.e., I cannot be concerned about redemption except as I am aware of myself in splitness and need, and, the possibility of fulfillment). But this moral awareness is more than the old-time "conviction for sin" as prerequisite to repentance; it includes a moral awareness of other selves.

All these, then, who are aware of sin and need, fulfillment, and the need to praise (Augustine has us confess *praise* as well as *sin*) ; those who are aware of self and selves, and of the great Thou and other thous, those who are veterans of meeting with this *Thou,* these come into the church. This is the communion of the saints, the fellowship of believers, the way, the body of Christ, the communion of the Holy Spirit and his work—which finds its common experience, locale, conviction, effect, and result, and its *raison d'être* in the life, teaching, death, resurrection, and coming of the Man Christ Jesus, unique Son of God and Saviour of the inhabited world of men.

In Jesus who is the Christ we experience the restoration from our estrangedness, and he, in the continuing power of the Holy Spirit (Troeltsch's *pneuma*-Christ), puts me in that relation with all selves which is salvation. By salvation we now mean everything God himself can do to make us whole persons. Those who are open to and are experiencing this being made whole live in the City of Light.

But we are not persons yet; we are in process still. This communion is the fellowship of those split ones who now are being annealed; the once-doomed are being re-deemed; but more; the redeemed are becoming redeemers themselves!

Look at this! My great teacher Carver drilled it into me: In the seventeenth of John, and elsewhere, the holy and blessed Trinity is the Father, the Son, and the Believer possessed of and by the Holy Spirit! I am redeemer, too—the means of other redemptions—and outside this church? Here Cyprian's *extra Ecclesiam nulla salus* is gospel.

This is why the church is like nothing else on the face of the earth; why it must never use the tools of the world for its gain; why it has to wait; why its members who are becoming persons have moral, ethical, relational, personal obligations. This is why its fellowship is like nothing else you have tasted —and this is why its oneness is holiness, its baptism is a death, its bread is a strengthening, its wine a toast to resurrection, the dust shaken off its feet a testimony to God and those who have heard, and its failure is a sacrament. This is why we die without its renewal.

But every hurt the church has got and every problem rises from who it is, where it is, and who its members are. The church is schizoid; its members are. The City of Light is city in the wilderness. Every place we ache stems from our calling to be City of God in the world where we are not. And every demand the gospel puts upon us, along with every tool we are given, is aimed at the recovery of persons in the church in and from and through the world for the sake of the personhood of all men.

III

The Communion of the Holy Spirit

There are two obvious implications in the title, *The Recovery of the Person.* The first is that someone is going to talk about the recovery of someone who has been lost and the second is that someone is to talk about the recovery of someone who has not been well. Both are justified suppositions. We are talking of the person who has been lost in and by the church and the one who was to have been made well in church and has not. Such miserable people in the churches! And church is no place to be recovered as one is, or discovered, or uncovered. Church has been for a thousand years a place to hide! Who would dare be himself in church? Church is where we go to be what we look like we are, or wish we were; it is never safe to be oneself in church!

Old-time westerner, all that is left of seventy years of drouth in West Texas, standing on his thin shanks and high boot heels on our beautiful slate floors, he took in arches, stained window, white marble altar, and the gorgeous hand-made French walnut pews with red cushions and end gates on the aisles. *Comment, at last:* "Man, you sure could hold a lot of sheep in here!"

THE RECOVERY OF THE PERSON

Answer: "We do, Joe, we do." And this is so. We are not persons in church; we are as sheep.

Those who work the university circuits frequently find their paths converging. Mine has met with that of the well-known research psychologist, Hobart Mowrer, three times this year. On the first campus I followed him and learned that he had offended the psychology people by claiming that psychiatry cannot heal since it can only relate a man to his own psyche. On the second he had alienated the religion people by claiming that the church cannot heal either because it has used justification by faith and the concept of grace to deny both personhood and responsibility. One discipline has lost guilt in guilt feeling, and the other has lost responsibleness in evasion. With both groups alienated by his preachments, I was prepared to find him about right when we ran together on the third campus. There is throbbing, aching truth in what he says. For where is there a healing?

If church is to be like nothing else on the face of the earth where and when is the healing? What and where is the communion of the Holy Spirit and the recovery of the person?

The Manful Spirit of the Holy

There is, says Wheeler Robinson, a self-emptying (*kenosis*) of God the Spirit that is a deeper humiliation to God than ever came in the emptying of God the Son. And this is what it means for God the Holy Spirit to take up his abode with us. This is what we mean when we speak of *persons as means of grace.* We mean that we meet God in each other. The manfulness of the holy One means that we can and do encounter the Eternal in the brother. When church is Church, life in church is *koinonia.*

Life in church is *koinonia* for both the "church-gathered"

and the "church-dispersed." Life in church is life-in-common wherever you are. It means to know as you are known; to be known utterly by one who calls you forth, whom you meet in the brother, before whom it is safe to "come as you are." The common life means the freedom, release to live through and behind our masks: The life one lives in the company of the glad is the life of the whole man, but who knows or sees the whole man? What church can or wishes to endure this!

Who sees the whole man? The doctor sees the organ or tissue of his specialty. The dentist sees mostly a mouth. The lawyer sees a litigant. The realtor sees only a prospect and may not know the tragedy that makes the seller sell. The mechanic, under the car, sees his client feet-to-knees at best. The undertaker does not see the whole man, he sees what is left of the whole man. The newsman sees only some extraordinary aspect that makes a man into news. The salesman looks only for the prospects, and so does the professional pastor. The white, provincial holy man looks only for the white, the provincial, and the pious. Who sees the whole man?

At eighty-four, sixty years a physician, stripped now of strength for his calling, from his hospital bed he berated me in affection: "You preachers! You always talk to a man born in 1879 who might live to 1964 as if he had no antecedents!"

The charge in the main is true. We forget how far behind a man the trail stretches. We act as if we were seeing the whole man, as if he could change by wishing to change. We forget that if it were not for society and what it has done to him, for history with what it remembers, he would be animal. And we are guilty of talking as if he had no problems and as if he had forever! We almost never see the whole man: how far his past, how high his desires, how deep his hurts, how great his needs, how dependent, hungry, frustrated; how great his cleavages, how broad his ambition, how vain his powers; how short his time, how presumptuous his claims, how real his death, how arrogant his projections. Who sees the whole man?

The French say he suffers from *"la déformation professionelle,"* he sees from the viewpoint of his own specialty; he is markedly blind outside it. He carries a swarm of convictions for comfort's sake, but, says Wilbur Urban, he has never been so knowing and unknowing, so purposed and purposeless, so disillusioned but victim of illusion. Threatened by dread, death, falseness, facelessness, and God's death, holding only some memories and ancient (now) techniques, he has been "trebly alienated" from God, nature, and his fellows. And what is as bad, most times his calling has so functionalized him that he is cut off from himself.

The holy may have gone altogether—his neuroses likely are willful neuroses, and face to face with life and its end, a man can no longer be justified in his work; he must find a justification within himself. So he falls into Unamuno's dread *gozarse uno la carne del alma* (he eats the flesh of his own soul) and hides behind his mask. In his young days he has three specific anodynes: habit, diversion, and work. He can chase a little ball or ride after hounds, he can join things, collect initials, work, hobby, play with stocks, insulate, divert, evade, raise chickens or roses until "he need not see the quality of his days." How each day sees buried a fragment of betrayed hopelessness. His impotence to heal much or bless for long is concealed in a salad ring of congealed gelatin. But now, in this weakness, his emptiness before God, the ladder to whose presence is gone, is before him. And he may have an added grief: even his relation with his dearest and best may be distorted by his professional deformation. He sees her clinically, biologically, according to his specialty. He diagnoses and prognosticates, and sometimes he can be proud that he is right; but he has lost the power to expect. Nothing he has met in his patients relieves him. They help weld his mask on. He is a priest, confessor, anodyne, Father, God, to the 60 per cent who really need another kind of help, and they help him by welding on his mask.

After days of this he comes home—to sleep by a cocked telephone, a restless sleep with six other people, and the mask is still on, and he cannot take it off. The Hebrew cry *Turn!* cannot reach him. I can not remove his mask and neither can he relieve himself of the plastered mold in which his soul is set.

And back of the mask? The real reason he is this; the primitive hungers, desires, and drives, and, as in my own calling, the bad motivations, the raw edges, the old, old shock, the impotency, the existential jolt, and the boy, the boy he was—and is.

How does one live with a man behind his mask? How does *koinonia* reach through these filters?

Someone must be able to become a hearer. Someone must recognize by hearing the inward flow of tears over guilt and a shame and the fears which are our "ecumenical sorrow." Someone must hear who knows the radical edges of human limitation so well that he can become the rest of someone. The hearing one joins him, and in the jointure leads the other to accept the irreducible dimensions of human life. In Buber's language your I calls forth his Thou by hearing— and it is worth a lifetime's waiting.

In this sense, *koinonia* requires us to be altar servers in the understanding that wherever the "acids of modernity," the erosions of human life, are being neutralized; wherever rest and restoration are happening; wherever he is being made whole and well, a man is in church. This is where religion happens and this is where he is religious—where and when the wasting away processes are reversed. This happens when his hunger and need become my burden and task. Here our wills merge and the mask is not torn away, it is heard through, and in the process something has happened to my mask:

I can stop manipulating; I can endure my rivals; I can quit

competing and proceed as need demands. I begin to taste a quality-relation; I have become the rest of someone, and in hearing I have been heard.

Koinonia is not to have all things in common. It is to know each other in common. The possessed is possessor, the given is giver, the heard is hearer, and the brother is a means of grace. This is the sovereign grace of God in persons that a man can be heard through anything, and once he has been heard he is really never again as if he had not been heard.

Everywhere the church tries to structure this, it ruins it. And everywhere the church forgets this hearing at the base of *koinonia* the structures it has raised for other valid purposes solidify to work against our being reminded. The endless treadmill of institutional repetitiveness deprives us of our nerve ends for hearing, and the redemption that is the point of the whole enterprise, the painful healing that is the goal of our enduring, is cut off.

What church can hope to house this man, his antecedents and his potential, along with the shaping healing Spirit of God and the meeting between them? And who wants *that* kind of church?

God does—now—here where we are. There is required in *koinonia* a willingness to allow the gospel to deal with the whole complex of modern life and living. Our antecedents for the last two hundred years have all but cut off the possibility of our being able to talk about our deepest crimes against the self. And, this thirty-year preoccupation with despair in the West, added to our sixteen-hundred-year-old preoccupation with sin add up to deny us the gospel insight that Jesus began where a fellow was and heard him past his sins in their context of need, hunger, blindness, paralysis. He began where a fellow was. That is to say, further, that *koinonia* requires a willingness to endure a gospel confrontation of the whole man—and this is painful as well as frightening. Man, in the context of his antecedents, his society, history, and biology (warts and all), is guilty, shamed, and frightened. Always he is these, and almost nowhere dare he, can he, tell about it. Nowhere, except in *koinonia,* and there, through the grace he meets in persons between whom the Holy Spirit has emptied himself, the God whose love makes him "vulnerable," to use the phrase of Daniel Day Williams, is encountered in very human form.

Such miserable people around the churches—waiting to be heard. Through the wicket gate the door that is opened and cannot be shut discloses a holy place where persons can happen—in church—in *koinonia,* in the meeting of hearers made able to hear through the divine emptying of self, the manful spirit of the Holy.

But quickly, lest it waste into another fad if left too long alone, lest our healing fellowship become litters of piglets suckling upon one another, or lest we make here and there a vampire who has never heard but feeds on bits of other person's moral and psychic vitals, let us look toward another arm of this healing—that commonwealth of value which we serve in

The Holy Spirit and the Manly

The Holy Spirit not only comes to church between and among persons, He conducts the service, he leads the dance, and this is more than *koinonia,* it is *leiturgia.* Church is always both. Look to the shape of your liturgy.

Although liturgy is always more than ritual, the latter is everywhere in life. Very early in some marriages the matter of the regular habitual performance of a certain sequence of acts impresses itself with a kind of horror and sameness on one partner or the other. "I'll have to live with this forever"; that glass of water by the bed, or the sequence of preparing for bed or arising, at mealtime, or going to work; the filling of a pipe, the way tea is served; or the manner, speed, and time of dressing, handling one's toast at breakfast, or like Linus, dragging one's blanket; the way he eats each vegetable by itself in sequence, the delays, the aimless actions, the wasted time. Many, perhaps most, marital frustrations express themselves through objection to some ritual. There is a hacking and objectionable ritual cough, or washing, or medicine taking, or the ritual of rolling a teen-ager's hair in curlers, or the ritual of her study to the blare of television, radio, telephone bells, and autos in and out of the drive. There is the ritual drink, and the ritual tardiness. Ritual marks every activity of living. It may even be that excessive regard for ritual makes bachelors. Certainly the rejection of a given ritual is a way of rejecting the person. After fifty years of marriage he still takes too long to wash, or shakes out his shoe before he puts it on as once he shook a boot to be sure no scorpion nested there in camp. You may as well leave him alone. It is a ritual, an act or series of acts regularly performed in the service of a particular end or value. He will not change it often. And everything we do is marked by ritual.

The point at which ritual becomes expressive of life's deepest meanings to us is the point at which ritual becomes *liturgy*. Ritual is the way of doing—the performance of rites. *Leiturgia* is the whole service and the server. Work, life work, is a service offered. It is liturgy. Ritual is the daily way of doing. Worship, a service representing the high values placed upon a relation, is *leiturgia*. Ritual is the way one does this. The *continuum* is the long haul, the High Mass, conducted around deep centers of concern and value—home, profession, church, marriage, parenthood. This is *leiturgia*: service offered to a value over the stretch of life. The way we go at this is ritual. *Discontinuum*, the going in and out, the processional-recessional, is *leiturgia*, too. The movement is liturgical in the context of its center and goal. The way the movement is conducted is a rite.

We all live our lives liturgically; there is no escape from liturgy. Life turns around our value reference points which seldom change in adulthood. The true meaning of your life to you can be read through your rituals performed in the service of your values. This is the shape of your liturgy. A true picture of your true service is a true picture of your values, and reveals the name of your God. We can tell the name of your God by the way you dance the dance of existence.

Living is art. Living is the execution of form in the service of need, value, and meaning. We make these forms, these movements, in a rhythm with our fellows, in concern for the time and season. Life is a dance we dance. There are tunes to which we all move: the dance of spring and of harvest, the dance at which all work in connection with a wedding, the ritual movements of the mother of the bride, for example; the more excited grandparent's dance in connection with the birth of a first grandchild; the dances of war, love, work, and the dance of waiting for the *danse macabre* to begin. There are tunes to which we move. How silly to protest it when even a protest is the next step in the dance we dance.

Add up all your ritual acts, motives, work, and the shape of your liturgy is crystal clear. One can tell in whose service he has lived by the dance he has danced, the ritual he has enacted, the liturgy he has shaped.

The commonwealth of value, to use Archbishop Temple's phrase, is a community dance, a tribal performance which draws a picture of its deepest values. There are no truly solo dances, no isolated selves, all are but momentary movements in the dancing of the whole, and the tribal dance is our true value structures symbolized. The shape of this liturgy may be power, or status, or acceptance, or diversion. But the tribe wears the brand, the symbol, it serves. The shape of our liturgy is the name for our God. Here our real values emerge. There can be no question about the dance part. Life requires it, to various tunes. Our purpose is to make our dance full of meaning worth enacting, but we are mostly ignorant dancers, content to recognize rhythm and tune, but not the meaning.

Life in *koinonia* where healing begins is life lived as liturgy. Our *leiturgia* is a common life offered up. Its shape is as a cross; its rhythm is as the heart beats; its content is the life offered up in communion; and its work is worship and its worship is its work. Gathered and dispersed, coming in and going out, rising and falling, the worship is the work. Worship: the witness of the whole church to its Lord, and what he does and has done, is always corporate, regular, orderly, liturgical, and ought to be like nothing else on the face of the earth. This is the salvation of the world; here the whole church, living and dead, comes alive in a present moment of response. There is no lone worshiping. We are summoned, we respond, we approach, we confess, we are absolved, we praise, we proclaim what he has done, we respond by offering up ourselves in work that is good work as the church dispersed. God comes to worship as Lord, Judge, God, and Grace. The preacher comes to worship as "prompter in the wings"; the people come to worship as doers in the drama of redemption which issues in the recovery of persons. But there is more. The healing of the nations requires more than *koinonia* and *leiturgia*. There is, everywhere the healing is at work, the issue of obedience:

The Company of the Obedient

There is also *diakonia*, the service of obedient men who live the *koinonia* life of *leiturgia*. Life in church, in the company of the obedient, is relation, communion, characterized by worship-work for the recovery of persons. And how is this service rendered? Given the communion that is *koinonia* and the worship that is *leiturgia,* the service of obedience which is *diakonia* proceeds first in:

Preaching-teaching. Somewhere on the road of performance all teaching spills over into preaching and vice-versa. Persons hear and answer. Preaching-teaching is always a conversation —it is dialogical—the preacher asks the questions—he does not mouth tired answers, or else the whole church cannot preach-teach. The congregation answers in mutters, or denial, or by saying, We do not understand you—a cheaper way of turning the head—or by acceptance. The whole church is involved in making persons, with the book, with our minds, our eager concern, and our experiences with the book, God, and each other.

The Ministry of Mercy is the proper use of advantage— the dispensing of our powers as persons—the cure of souls. Here the whole community assumes responsibility for the ripening of its members as persons. The shepherding is in the hands of the flock—even the shearing. We are obligated to be well; and more, to be well *made.*

Vocation-Response: The witness of the whole to and as a whole is stewardship over our powers and gifts. It is the faithful service of the call to witness—we are the evangel—and are evangelists. This is no mere function, but the ablative *dimension* of witness. We are not proprietors but guests with an obligation for having come at all, yet at home enough to be called upon—and our response is aimed to bless the city and the world. *Urbe et orbe,* the Pope says, as he turns to benediction, and so do we.

This community of persons-becoming-persons that is the church has various forms, but its situation is the same in the world. *It always has what it wants.* It always has exactly what it wants. It does not have what it says it wants—but what it does have in its corporate life is a reflection of what it has truly wanted.

For example, if a church ever wanted renewal it could have this. But it would have to want it. If the church desires ("With desire I have desired to eat this passover with you," the Teacher said) ; if the church *desires* the power of the Holy Spirit, He comes. Since Chrysostom, in the Greek church, they have said two or three would bring him. But we never have the Holy Spirit at our disposal. In church we do not pray to have more of the Spirit; we pray that the Holy Spirit may have his informing, rebuking, cauterizing, authoritative, redeeming way in the lives of persons in the church.

Veni Spiritu Sanctu!

and it is a prayer.

Meanwhile, was it not "on the night in which he was betrayed" that "Jesus took bread, and blessed, and brake it, and gave to them, and said, Take, eat: this is my body. . . . And he took the cup . . ." and look—in this context of betrayal— as always, what giants-to-be, what persons were at table with him.

There is a meeting of minds between the high priests of the age that says the answer to the question of our destiny is "written in the wind." That is to say, the matter is determined outside the reach of our energy, competency, and responsibleness. As the ballad has it:

> How many roads must a man walk down, before they
>   call him a man? . . .
> The answer is written in the wind.

Is it now? Is it written in the wind, the sand, among the stars? Is it engraved in the swirling tides of chance, fate, mystery, luck, Allah, God Almighty, glands, genes, body

Chemistry? Or is there perhaps a thing we may have missed?

Many powers have united to say the answer is not in our hands. Among these, respectable histories, biologies, theologies, psychologies, and sociologies have proclaimed our lack of responsibility. There is a very real sense in which the two great streams of modern theology join with the basic insight of twentieth-century psychiatry to deny us real responsibility. Freud never saw Schleiermacher or Barth, nor would Barth and Schleiermacher like the association, but they are representatives, with Freud, of a great three-horse hitch—a troika —that has raced the modern mind into a *cul-de-sac* that denies us our competent existence. And these are not alone. The new universe, since Einstein, is at best no place for the indulgence of our romantic notions of sheer freedom. The net result of our questing in the twentieth century seems to indicate that, insofar as a view of man is concerned, Barth's man is *depraved;* Schleiermacher's man is *dependent;* Freud's man is *determined;* Marx's man is *driven;* the man of Dewey's interpreters has seemed totally *conditioned;* and the man of Pavlov is a slobbering *reactor to stimuli.* They join the chorus of the ballad—*the answer is written in the wind*—some wind beyond our turning. The newest baby of them all joins theology, philosophy, psychology, and biochemistry to put it in sociological lingo—any answer is written in the winds of social laws beyond our referendum or powers of recall. We have no franchise here.

Is religion an "opiate of the people"? They are all opiates, tranquilizers, depressants, when they turn mankind from the divine *Imago* of his own responsibleness. No wonder the modern world has turned its back on reason and our powers of the rational.

Hobart Mowrer, who has shocked many by his claim that neither Freud nor faith can heal, did not go far enough! Any kind of faith that diverts us to an answer written in the wind, to a current in which we can put no responsible oar, is a denier of our *humanum*, destiny, being. The answer is not written in the wind—it lies in the realization of the person-hood we are called by God to achieve.

That the church least of all has understood this is patently so. That the church last of all will recognize its healing powers is probably so. But the answer is not in the winds, nor in the fiber strings of our cellular body architecture. The answer is in our laps, the lap of our responsible hearing and doing.

The recovery of open love—*koinonia*—and the recovery of open relation—*leiturgia*—participate now in a third—the recovery of obedient will. This is *diakonia*—the life of the obedient will.

When Freud, in 1917, forecast the coming revolution in anthropology, it rested on his dictum, "The ego is not master in its own house. . . . the conscious mind is mastered from behind it!" Freud was as great a shock to that psychology which had held consciousness and psyche to be the same, as was his predecessor Schopenhauer a shock to that classical philosophy which had held intellect and reason to be the center. But Schopenhauer may have the better of it. Although his will is to mind and reason a moral threat quite as powerful as that threat to reason implicit in an amoral id at center, in either case the rational is ruled by life from behind. Had we a choice, who would not prefer to be guided by a moral will rather than by a ruthless and careless id? Even if the will is sick, it may still be more nearly redeemable than naked id. For will, at center, can be appealed to on moral and responsible grounds. Is the world responsible will, with an idea? Then what is the great idea? In various guises it has appeared among us, but F. D. Maurice knew it and pressed it on the English Unitarians, "You are under the law to love, you know you are, and you have been fighting against it." And so we have.

If it is fair to allow the mores and patterns of our living to serve as a manifestation of our dogma, then Hobart Mowrer has read Protestantism correctly when he claims that salvation by grace, unearned merit, faith alone, are slogan tranquilizers that have deprived us of our responsibilities. These have been used as excusers to evade our real humanity by relieving us of a guilt that can only be discharged from its awful function by our open confession, not only to God, but *to each other*. From the way we have lived, one would not be really unfair to claim that salvation by grace relieves us too easily of our liabilities. Hence, the church has done no better than psychiatry at this healing business.

But what if there is a law? A law to love, a law that demands openness and communion, a law that can be realized only in that communion of guilt, confession, acceptance, and obedience which comes to pass in a healing community? And what if this law to love in the open is really a grace of God? What if *all* law that is law is really grace? What if there has never been any true conflict between law and grace, since even the fundamental Ten Commandments rest on a grace-filled "Hear, O Israel, the Lord our God is one . . . And thou shalt love the Lord thy God." Does this not change things?

Mowrer is both right and wrong. And under either rubric the church is guilty.

You have been heard to say that you would love to love Christ, but the church is in your way. The church as it has been is almost always in the way. Yet this church which is not yet church is *us*. And if it is ever church, it will still be *us*. But when it becomes church, it will be composed of a "we" who have discovered our destiny, not as written in the wind, but as resting on the law to love, hear, and do, which is God's great grace at work. Nor is it strange that a contemporary Jewish theologian under 35 should be the one to remind us that the Israel of God is a realm of law only as it is true that all law which is law is the grace of the Holy One.

167

It is not written in the wind. It is written in the grace of that God whose law to love provides a healing place for our wills in a community of responsible, open, confessing and loving; and this is the ethic of obedience. Its biblical name is *diakonia*, the company of obedient wills.

Christian unity begins in the unity of the human race. This is given and gotten. One does not join the human race easily. His ego drives him apart in himself. He seeks his own and his own world. His voices are his own. Yet, however dimly, he is aware of other voices and the Voice. He joins the race at the point where he begins to hear. He becomes Christian at the point where Jesus Christ is heard and obeyed. He will teach us for what we are to listen!

That is to say, this Christian community lives between persons in relation. This becomes almost instantly ethical. To hear is an ethical act because it involves also a willingness to do in the light of what one has heard.

Christian community never begins in "I have something to say." Nor can it begin in "I have something to do." It begins in a hearing that is willed and proceeds in "radical obedience" to the demand of the High Good in the heard situation.

To hear is to be changed; to hear is to answer with acts. But what does one obey? The voice he hears, or the need of which the voice speaks, or yet another? The answer is, all these. All voices house a need, he feels for this; and what he does, is done in response to both that sensed need and the higher voice he hears in Jesus Christ. This is how Christian community transcends the merely human and becomes personal and Christian. For in Jesus who is the Christ the relatedness becomes a community on which we can rely. It becomes safe to have heard and to emerge. Here we get together, at the point of hearing and doing.

And what does one do? He does the highest he knows in the light of his hearing of Jesus Christ and the need he hears.

168

In this he finds himself also heard even before he has spoken. Acceptance is a fact for him—a fact of relation. The encounter continues. We are at one in hearing and doing.

The answer to Mowrer is not an assent to his denial of justification by grace; rather, it lies in the discovery that the law of our own responsibility for hearing and doing *is* free grace—the grace of a freedom limited only by our guilt, not our finiteness, which guilt can be dealt with only by that grace-filled discovery of a gracious acceptance by other guilt-ridden men who constitute the responsible hearers and doers of the law to love. This is the healing church. Its responsibility is a grace; its work of hearing and doing is grace—and the grace-filled ethic of this obedience is in our hands or it is no grace, for it is not yet given. In the grace-filled law of my own being in responsible agency there is constituted a community of hope in which, participating, we matter, eternally. And this is no writing in the wind. It is graven in our hearts by creation in the heart of God.

How many roads must a man walk down, before they will call him a man? And how many chances, how many new roads do you think you will see? And how many times can a man start again from the beginning? Why, living is like space flying. You do it the first time, or not at all!

Hoyt Nance has reminded me of *The Proud and the Profane,* a play in which the widow of World War times becomes obsessed to know how well or how poorly her timid husband had died. She comes at length to his resting place and finds a brooding veteran of her husband's destroyed army acting as gravekeeper to his dead companions. "Yes, he knew her husband as well as any—and how did he die? Why he died like an *amateur,* just like all the rest."

And so do we. We are amateurs at dying *and* at living— and for amateurs there is one road, go as it will. We make it here or not at all.

Here is where we have to have each other. And this is why love is a law. Only this can constitute a company of the glad for such a pilgrim journey to be once—made—forever. For here, where the insertion of the vehicle in its orbit is a matter of going out of this world, a whole company of competence is required. How sad to find the road so thronged with mobs who know neither the origin nor the destiny, nor even the company for their journey. We are all amateurs here, and we need each other, for the answer we seek is not written in a wind, it is by law and by God written in the heart of my neighbor whom I have to hear and know in order to find my way on a journey to be once made forever.

And this is why you will never escape your need for church. There is no place to go other than to the church in your house among your fellow travelers, and here is your means of becoming person. Persons are means of grace; means of grace are ways God meets us; God meets us between and in persons who are hearing, doing, and obeying, and therefore are redeeming powers between darkness, splitness, and the light. Wherever this happens, guilt is being atoned, persons are being made whole, the Christ has appeared, and a journey is a journey to the light.

And the way? Not written in the winds. It is in the neighbor's heart and in my own where God dwells and where the church comes alive between us as the community of open love, relation, and obedience to the light we have. And when you are found by this, who knows what new knowledge of life and universe and of God there will be?

For Henri Breuil, we have "just cast off the last moorings which held us to the neolithic age." For Pierre Teilhard de Chardin, what we are up against is "the heavy swell of an unknown sea which we are just entering from behind the cape that protected us." We are all like those first compelled and timid Phoenician voyagers who ventured beyond Gibraltar —we have to find our courage in each other where the

170

"same leaky bottom in these wild waters bears us all." And movingly, achingly, in the ability to love, relate, and obey, we discover where God dwells between us here in our journey into communion.

It matters tremendously that we should know that the journey matters; that at the price of our enduring and struggling a giant stride is being taken; that something gigantic is coming off in our time in the process of man-realization. And the hope—God's hope—in our hands, is that we can recognize ourselves as part of all that coheres, co-exists, and shall sense with joy the sweep of a movement whose path comprehends all that we ask or think or seek or remember or regret or repent or need or hope in such a fashion that the journey is infinitely worthwhile, for it leads to a Father's house.

Meanwhile, on the road, it is enough to know ourselves as sons in the company of our brothers on our way to a personhood in a communion that has been constituted and invaded by his great grace.

Note Section

page line

27 1   *Weimar 1803*, by Otto Knille, is reproduced in color as a frontispiece for
         Volume II of *The German Classics of the Nineteenth and Twentieth Cen-
         turies*, ed. Francke (New York: The German Publication Society, 1913).

28 8   Excerpted from the last entry in Eckermann's diary, *Words of Goethe*
         (New York: Classic, 1933), p. 394.

29 2   Thomas Mann, *Essays* (New York: Vintage Books, 1957).

31 15   This remark is not mine but that of an Episcopal clergyman unknown
         to me.

38 4, 9 Baillie, *Our Knowledge of God* (New York: Charles Scribner's Sons, 1939),
         pp. 7, 17.

47 12   Rauschenbusch, *A Theology for the Social Gospel* (Nashville: Abingdon
         Press, Apex reprint), pp. 48, 49, 174-75.

51 30   From a letter by Professor Joseph Barnhart, then a graduate student in
         philosophy at Boston University.

52 6   Barth is particularly careful not to attribute need to God in *The
         Humanity of God* (Richmond, Va.: John Knox Press, 1960), *passim*.

52 15   Barth's section on *The Being of God as the One Who Loves*, II/1, pp.
         272-97, is crucial here; especially see p. 296.

52 19   Barth, *Dogmatics*, II/1, p. 291.

52 29   These words are particularly apt as a characterization of Barth's theme in
         Christ and Adam. The words which stay in my mind may, however, be
         the words of Mackintosh in *Types of Modern Theology*, p. 299.

53 3   Barth, *The Word of God and the Word of Man*, tr. Horton (New York:
         Harper Torchbook, 1957), p. 196.

53 10   See Barth, *Dogmatics*, IV/1 (57.3) "The Fulfillment of the Broken
         Covenant," pp. 67-78. But better than the phrase "change of parts," which
         is that of Mackintosh, is Barth's own use of the word "exchange"; e.g.,
         five times in less than a page of type (pp. 75-76). Also see any Barth
         discussion of *imputatio*.

53 35   Which Barth affirms ahead of all critics.

54 24   See *Dogmatics* II/1, p. 291.

55 16   *Ibid.*, p. 296.

56 13   *Ibid.*, pp. 284 ff.

56 22   E. Bohl, *Dogmatik* (1887), p. 61, as cited by Barth, *Dogmatics* II/1, p.
         282.

58 7   As cited by Mann, *Essays*, p. 314. Barth also cites this aphorism of
         Silesius in slightly different form (II/1, p. 281).

58 32   *Ibid.*, pp. 313-14.

59 11   *Ibid.*, p. 315.

65 14   Barth, *Christ and Adam*, tr. Small (New York: Harper & Row, 1957), p.
         14.

69 —   Pierre Teilhard de Chardin, *The Divine Milieu* (New York: Harper &
         Row, 1960), p. 15.

71 11   Rauschenbusch, *A Theology for the Social Gospel*, p. 42.

71 30   *Ibid.*, p. 5.

76 19   *Ibid.*, p. 102.

79 6   The words are cited by Mann, *Essays*; but see Eckermann, *Words of
         Goethe*, p. 128, and several passages in Goethe's *Elective Affinities*.

80	3	Biblically in the Elijah saga, in *The Revelation,* and also in Ignatius.
81	18	(After "person.") As early as his 1926 talks on Schleiermacher, Barth paraphrases Schleiermacher: "All existence of God in the world is mediated through Christ," in Barth, *Theology and Church* (New York: Harper & Row, 1962), p. 188.
81	31	This is the famous *nichtkenner* of death and *verkenner* of evil with which Hans Ehrenberg disposes of Feuerbach's man as God. Ehrenberg is cited by Barth at this point in both his articles in English on Feuerbach: (ch. 7 of *Theology and Church,* and his beautiful introduction to a reprint of Feuerbach's *The Essence of Christianity*).
83	13	H. R. Mackintosh, *Types of Modern Theology* (New York: Charles Scribner's Sons, 1945), p. 51.
83	14	Otto, in *The Idea of the Holy,* pp. 146-47, credits Schleiermacher with claiming that religious *intuitions* can truly grasp and experience the "overplus" which "cannot be apprehended by mere theoretic cognition of the world." Otto also edited an edition of *The Discourses* in which, he says, he aimed to carry his estimate of Schleiermacher forward.
83	29	Mackintosh, *Types of Modern Theology.*
88	17	William Temple, *Nature, Man and God* (New York: The Macmillan Company, 1951), pp. 35-41.
88	18	See Étienne Gilson, *The Christian Philosophy of St. Thomas Aquinas* (New York: Random House, 1956), pp. 59-83.
93	30	In *Complete Poetry and Selected Prose of John Donne* (New York: Modern Library), p. 489.
94	30	Barth, *The Humanity of God,* p. 50.
95	15	Irenaeus, *Against Heresies* II.24.4 in *Ante-Nicene Fathers,* tr. Roberts and Donaldson (Buffalo: 1887), I, 391, 448.
95	18	*Ibid.*
95	24	*Ibid.,* p. 428.
96	1	*Ibid.,* p. 448.
96	9	*Ibid.,* p. 428.
99	16	Dom Gregory Dix, *Jew and Greek* (London: Dacre Press, 1953), p. 5.
124	25	Carl Sandburg, "Wilderness," from *The Cornhuskers.*
125	1	Huxley, *The Uniqueness of Man,* from *Man Stands Alone* by Julian Huxley (Harpers) is the source of any technical language used in this section.
125	8	Sandburg, "Wilderness."
125	26	*Ibid.*
126	14	*Ibid.*
126	28	*Ibid.*
127	19	*Ibid.*
128	9	*Ibid.*
131	18	*Ibid.*
134	20	Mann, *Essays,* p. 301.
135	12	*Don Quixote,* as cited by Mann, *ibid.,* p. 354.
143	8	Private correspondence from John N. DeFoore, entire poem.
145	5	Dylan Thomas, "Do not go gentle into that good night."
146	25	Kierkegaard.
155	1	The term has found its current usage through Reuel Howe.
155	21	The accuser here was the widely respected head of Duke Foundation, Dr. Watt Rankin, from whom a journeyman pastor has gotten other insights as well.
153	18-24	See William Barrett, *Irrational Man* (New York: Doubleday & Co., Inc., 1958), p. 99. And see Pascal.
159	6	A sermon, as preached at Union Theological Seminary, "The Vulnerable and the Invulnerable God," printed in *Union Seminary Quarterly Review,* XVII (March, 1962), pp. 223-29.

Index